Betty Joyce

What a special Rose Rose! you are to Him. Keep trusting!

Love
Mercy Akpan
May 2003

Mercy Beyond Measure

By

Mercy Akpan

© 2002 by Mercy Akpan. All rights reserved.

No part of this book may be reproduced, stored in a retrieval system, or transmitted by any means, electronic, mechanical, photocopying, recording, or otherwise, without written permission from the author.

ISBN: 1-4033-1595-7 (e-book)
ISBN: 1-4033-1596-5 (Paperback)

This book is printed on acid free paper.

Dedication

To my sons Emem E. Akpan and Otu E. Akpan. You are a blessing to me. Your faith, courage, and strength are God given. Wear them throughout your sojourn for it pleases God. To my husband and friend Essien W. Akpan.

Acknowledgements

To my heavenly Father for it is all by His grace.

To my brothers: Emmanuel O. Etim, Otu Etim Oku, and Edmund E. Oku.

To my sisters: Iquo T.W. Inyang, Alice E. Nkemedi, and the late Akon O. Etim. Your prayers and weekly phone calls across the miles meant so much.

Many Thanks to:

All who sacrificed through prayers, visits, and gifts contributed to this gift of grace. God knows who you are and even though your names are not mentioned be assured that God is blessing you. If all names are mentioned I will exhaust the paper. God who sees and knows all things will reward you openly.

In Loving Memory...

Of my father Chief/Elder Otu Etim Oku and my mother Nkoyo Otu Etim Oku; a virtuous woman. The best parents in the whole world, and I thank God for the privilege of being your daughter.

It has been a privilege to be Mercy Otu-Etim Akpan's pastor for she is a person who accepts change, the will of God, and who has been proven in God through her many sufferings, having faced the spectre of bone cancer and having come out victorious.

I have encouraged her to make her testimony known to those who are the Body of Christ as well as those who know not Christ that they might be able to see how the Grace of God is sufficient and as His strength is made perfect in weakness and to let them know that cancer has to bow down before the name of Jesus. For God is able to get the Glory out of all situations for He said not to give thanks for everything, but in everything.

Sister Mercy is the one who has given thanks in the darkest times of her life.

Yeah, though she walked through the Shadows of death, the promise of fearing no evil was revealed through her situation. She is a living cancer- free testimony that cancer is as a common cold to the God of the universe and I thank her for allowing me to give this forward and count it as a privilege in the Master's Service.

Pastor Edred A. Black Founder of Grace Community Church of God in Christ in Worcester Massachusetts.

The Lord is my Shepherd; I shall not want.

He maketh me to lie down in green pastures:
He leadeth me beside the still waters.

He restoreth my soul: he leadeth me in the paths of righteousness for his name's sake.

Yea, though I walk through the valley of the Shadows of death, I will fear no evil; for thou are with me; thy rod and thy staff they comfort me.

Thou preparest a table before me in the presence of my enemies: thou anointest my head with oil; my cup runneth over. Surely goodness and mercy shall follow me all the days of my life: and I will dwell in the house of the Lord forever.

—Psalm 23:1-6

Table of Contents

Introduction xvii

Divine Assignment 1

My Life before Grace 10

Membership at Grace Community Church 13

Don't Despise Prophecies: The Diagnosis 19

Second Opinion 32

Resisting the Devil 42

Divine Prescription 54

Other Attacks 58

His Personal Appearance 63

Obedience Is Better Than Sacrifice 70

The Call to Wake Up 80

Healing through the Stripes of Jesus! 89

At Home 104

Chemotherapy/Infusion Center: Nightingales 108

Mental Warfare 111

Guard Your Healing: Affliction Will Not Return Twice 164

Conclusion 173

Appendix A 179

Appendix B 187

Introduction

What should you do when you come face-to-face with a mountain that looks too rugged to climb? Your heartbeat rate doubles. At that moment, it is impossible to strategize a method to get to the top.

The mountain is cancer. The mountain is the devil, there to steal, kill, and destroy. The mountain is a mass of lies. The mountain is Goliath, and you are David. You must do exactly what David did: Face Goliath with confidence. God did not give us the spirit of fear; He gave us power, love, and a sound mind. David relinquished all to God, for the battle is the Lord's.

Wipe your tears, gather yourself together, and rest on His bosom, "for [He is] the Lord that healeth thee" (Exod. 15:26). Thoughts will begin to flood your mind as answers are sought. Disbelief and shock will kiss each other; both will make confusion a masterpiece. Helplessness and loss of control will by no means be absent. All human options will dwindle and diminish. Throughout it all, however, one thing will be sure and standeth true: the Word of God.

God is our refuge and strength, a very present help in trouble.

Therefore will not we fear, though the earth be removed, and though the mountains be carried into the midst of the sea;

Though the waters thereof roar and be troubled, though the mountains shake with the swelling thereof.

God is in the midst of her; she shall not be moved: God shall help her, and that right early.

Be still, and know that I am God: I will be exalted among the heathen, I will be exalted in the earth.

The Lord of hosts is with us; the God of Jacob is our refuge. (Ps. 46:1-3, 5, 10-11)

Divine Assignment

Mercy beyond Measure was birthed at a moment of pain, high fever, restlessness, and a certain degree of anguish and frustration. I was almost in a fetal position one minute, and supine the next minute. A small soft voice spoke, "Write a book. I have brought you out for others to know and experience my love and compassion and believe my Word."

Yea, though I walk through the valley of the shadow of death, I will fear no evil: for thou art with me; thy rod and thy staff they comfort me. (Ps. 23:4)

One early morning the Holy Spirit quickened me to write this book and gave me the title. A few months later, God confirmed this through my pastor. The urgency to write this book is indescribable. The Holy Sprit has brought things to my remembrance, thereby encouraging and motivating my writing. Such urgency has been rare—even when I was unprepared for a fast-approaching final exam.

There is nothing as compelling as fulfilling a divine appointment! Also, when someone has been kind and good to you, you want to share this kindness with other people. In this instance, however, it is not just an ordinary kindness; this is a very special kindness from the most faithful, special, and truthful person. He has mandated me to tell this story.

Do not pass it; it is valuable for such a time as we are now facing. This is shalom, peace—nothing missing, and nothing broken. This is the gift of eternal life, salvation, redemption, and faith. It is an internal and external makeover. God wants you to know that you are not alone! God can heal physically and spiritually. We are all his children, and his thoughts concern us all. God longs for us to depend on him through his beloved Son, Jesus. Our daily communion and fellowship breed intimacy with our Lord, and this is where we come to hear his voice and know his awesome promises for us. Come and let us drink from the fountain of life. Hallelujah! The training goes on.

What I am about to share with you comes from the bottom of my heart and is as true as the Bible is true. As they say, "Experience is the best teacher." Glory to God! It is my belief that before God's children go through situations or are confronted with tribulations, God prepares us through visions, prophesies, dreams, and Scriptures. Sometimes we heed the warning; other times, we miss it.

For my own experience, the Holy Spirit had ministered to me about diet and rest, at least a couple of years before the eruption. I remember one occasion clearly. The Holy Spirit spoke to me while I was driving, advising me to eat lots of vegetables and also to set specific times for my meals, rather than eating on the run. I also needed to rest. The love of God is awesome and faithful. Yes, the warning or advice was given, but the choice to obey was up to me, and I procrastinated for one reason or another. God will prepare you spiritually, physically, and emotionally for what you are going to go through. After all, He is omnipotent (all-powerful) and omniscient (all-knowing). I grew up believing in

God but did not have or build an intimate individualized relationship with him, my heavenly Father, my Creator, my Maker. I prayed on the run and in a hurry. Never gave a thought on mortality—not a thought! The following song was given to me in a dream shortly before those fiery darts of the devil struck. It represents God's continuous tenderhearted and nurturing nature toward us.

> It Is Me! Hallelujah!
>
> It Is Me! Hallelujah!
>
> I Have Loved You
>
> I Have Protected You
>
> I Sent You Here
>
> Yes, It Is Me
>
> *(Repeat three times.)*

I made excuses not to sing the song, because I was living in an apartment and did not want to disturb my neighbors. With these excuses going through my mind, I heard a voice say, "You remain awake because I do not want you to forget this song." I lay there with those words melodiously echoing and reechoing in my mind until 5:30 A.M., when I received the mandate to sing the song out loud—so I did. He is my Creator, my Maker, and provides for me. He wanted me to know that He keeps charge over me no matter where I am; that He sent me at the beginning and has been protecting me ever since; and that, in health or sickness, He is with me. Hallelujah! That is how our heavenly Father beholds all of us if we come to him and allow him to take care of us.

Mercy Beyond Measure

The second instance of God's warning as to what I would be facing occurred during the summer of 1994. I was in church attending a Tuesday evening Bible teaching, which my pastor elder, Edred A. Black, conducted. At the end of Bible teaching, the pastor made an altar call, in which people go to the altar for prayer. I did not go out for prayer on this particular day, but God saw me and sent a message through my pastor: "Sister Margaret, God said to tell you that the devil is going to try to put something on you, but He also said to tell you not to worry, for He (God) will bring you out." I did not quite understand what this meant—to be exact, I did not understand what I would be *brought out from*. Nevertheless, I was very thankful to God for his promise. One particular thought did flash briefly through my mind. I thought that the devil was going to attack me financially so that it would be impossible for me to go ahead with a business venture I was anticipating at the time.

God's third warning about what I would be facing came through a dream. I found myself in the middle of a huge fenced-in ditch filled with skeletal remains. An elderly white male, approximately sixty to seventy years old, sat on a chair beside the only exit. His hair was gray, and he had a beard to match. I walked from the center of the ditch among the dry bones to where the man was sitting. I greeted him, and he asked me what I needed. I informed him that I wanted to get out of the ditch to the other side but that the fence was too high for me to climb.

Immediately he got up to help me. As he picked me up, I lifted my eyes and, behold, my husband was standing outside the fence. I extended my arms toward my husband, who got a hold of my arms and upper body, and I landed safely on the outside. I thanked the old man through the fence, and the dream ended.

My Life before Grace

Born to a Presbyterian elder and a virtuous woman, as depicted in Proverbs 31:10, morning and evening devotions were imperative and mandatory. We were taught to know, believe, and trust God as the Truth, the Way, and the Life. Attending Sunday school was a must, after which my father would ask me what I had learned. I had to summarize the day's sermon to him. Therefore, it was important for me to pay attention at Sunday school and at church service. I honestly can equate my father with Joshua: "For me and my house, we will serve the Lord" (Josh. 24:15).

My father was a devout man of God, not only by words but also by precepts and examples. To my father, Bible reading and studying were his daily nourishment. He ate the Word and made the Word his water. He would often refer to the Bible as the *Book of Life*. As a customary court judge and a chief, all his counsel was beset on biblical principles. When he was at home, people sought his counsel, and God blessed him with wisdom, understanding, and revelation knowledge.

Thank you, Lord, for having sent me to this man and woman who taught me about you. "Train up a child in the way he should go: and when he is old, he will not depart from it" (Prov. 22:6).

After I left home, I designed a perfect configuration for my life. I call it my *life wheel*. In the center of this wheel, I chose *speed* as my catalyst. My life was in my own hands, so I devised my own compass. During this self-centeredness, I dictated time. I did everything in a hurry. I even prayed in a hurry; my prayer consisted of Psalms 1, 23, and 121, and the Lord's Prayer. I recited these psalms, which I call my *nurturing and foundational psalms* because my father incorporated them into our daily morning and evening devotions. I added Psalm 51 on my own: I came across it; I read it; and I liked it; so I added it to my foundational-psalms collection. The belief and the fear of the Lord were well founded in me before I left home, but I had not cultivated an intimate relationship with my heavenly Father and the Lord Jesus. In 1992, all this was destined to change through God's love by his Son, Jesus Christ. To God be the glory!

Membership at Grace Community Church

A friend invited me to visit her church. I accepted the invitation and went on a Sunday. I had a wonderful time, and what I experienced aided in my returning there. The pastor taught from the Bible and quoted Scriptures, and some of the members would complete the Scripture with him (per his encouragement). I wanted to hear more and to be a part of this body of Christ. I always enjoyed memorizing Shakespearean plays and the like, so I decided to pledge membership at the Grace Community Church of God in Christ.

I attended Tuesday Bible teachings and Friday deliverance service. I could not wait for these days to approach. I took notes, read them at home, and referred to the Scriptures. To me it was like an assignment.

My pastor emphasized reading and studying the Word of God. He would add, "This is the only way you would know for yourself." The Holy Spirit prompted me to immerse and meditate myself in the Word of God. The more I read the Bible, I became hungry and thirsty for more. I wanted to consume everything about my heavenly Father.

I started reading and studying the synoptic Gospels. The first three of the four Gospels of the New Testament are called the *synoptic Gospels* because they give general views of Christ's life. The Fourth Gospel (the Gospel of John) is called the *Doctrinal Gospel* because it teaches specifically the doctrine of the divine nature of Christ as the Son of God.

Mercy Beyond Measure

Even though I had read some of the Bible as a little girl and had studied the synoptic Gospels (Matthew, Mark, Luke) and the Doctrinal Gospel (John)—plus the Book of Acts in high school—I took my pastor's advice as a prophet and devoted time to read and study the Bible. When I came to Matthew 6:33, something rose up inside of me: "But seek ye first the Kingdom of God, and his righteousness; and all these things shall be added unto you." I began to sense a deep desire to draw close to God. Something peaceful and beautiful was taking a hold of me. Nothing else motivated me; every ambition, goal, and aspiration had shifted from self-centeredness to God-centeredness.

One day, this prayer simply rolled out: "Lord, I know there are levels in you. I picture those levels as a river, and I'm dipping my cup from the top to the bottom. As my cup is being filled, I'm asking you to ensure that I do not miss any ingredients in each layer. Help me to drink it all." Then I added, "Father, teach me as you taught the apostle Paul, and also teach me how to praise and worship you as King David did."

This prayer did not come from my inquiring mind. It was God through the Holy Spirit. I meant it then, and I mean it now. This incorruptible diploma is worth studying for, and I pray that the learning continues until I behold His face.

Regardless of where you are, empty your heart and give yourself to God—total self-abandonment to the utmost, depending completely on God, realizing that on your own you can do nothing. Through your helplessness, you begin to trust your heavenly Father; as you experience him, you will love, depend on, and believe in him. Here faith begins.

Beloved, whether your church is a cathedral liken to Saint Peter's Basilica, or a storefront church, what matters most to Christ Jesus is the heart. Our heart is the church of God. God will speak through his prophets and the Bible in either of these churches. The pastor must be committed to God and must be entrusted to care for His flock. He must be anointed as well as filled by the Holy Ghost. You must be obedient toward His teachings. The church must be alive, stirring toward God's righteousness and holiness. "Thou wilt show me the path of life: in thy presence is fullness of joy; at thy right hand there are pleasures for evermore" (Ps. 16:11).

After I received the baptism of the Holy Spirit, my pastor made a very profound and lasting statement to me: "Sister Margaret, I heard that you received the gift of the Holy Spirit. One thing I must tell you is that when you start speaking in tongues, the devil really goes wild. So you must stay in prayer."

This type of divine advice surpasses all monetary value. He gave me an eternal piece of advice, and I shall cherish it as long as I live. It helped prepare and equip me for the volcanic eruption that was to follow. Pastor Black, please remain connected to God for Him to continue to use you.

Don't Despise Prophecies: The Diagnosis

The manifestation of the 1994 prophesy, through Pastor Black, came in 1995. My right hand (upper-arm area) and right shoulder started hurting terribly that winter. The pain was intense and continuous. I went to see a chiropractor who had treated me for an unrelated pain. He proceeded to treat my arm. I kept going for treatment, but my right arm became extremely painful, so I asked him to refer me to a doctor for an X ray, MRI, or bone scan.

The referral performed an MRI on me, and the result was promised within a couple of days. By the next scheduled treatment, the result had been sent to him. When I arrived for the appointment that morning, I sat down and started reading a magazine. Suddenly I heard this: "Get up, and go take a look at your chart." I had never done this before, but I immediately got up and got my chart. Attached to the front was the result of the MRI. Two typed pages. I read through it and put it back just as it was.

The chiropractor finally came out and was friendly as usual. He took the report of the MRI and told me that there was nothing to worry about. I asked him what he meant. He said that the result of the MRI was not bad. "Oh really?" I asked. He answered, "Yeah." Then I said, "Did you read the second page?" He again responded, "Yeah."

At that point, I asked for the report, which he handed to me. I informed him that I knew that a lesion on the bone, which indicates *some form of lymphoma*—as the wording of the report stated—

Mercy Beyond Measure

was by no means an indication that "there was nothing to worry about."

With that note, I left his practice and concluded that he was not at all caring. I went home and called for an appointment to see my primary physician. A few days after my call, I saw the doctor, in hand with a copy of the MRI report. Within a few minutes of my visit, I was referred to see an oncologist the next day.

I drove myself to this first appointment, totally clueless of what was ahead of my family and me. I reported to the receptionist, who told me to have a seat. There were about seven or eight people in the waiting room, reading and flipping through different magazines. About fifteen minutes later, my name was called.

After being weighed, I was placed in a room. A few minutes later, a man walked in and introduced himself as an oncologist. He looked quiet and somewhat depressed, with some heaviness about him. He sat down and asked me a few questions about my family medical history. He then explained that he needed to draw fluid from my spinal column. I asked him if the procedure would be painful, to which he responded no. Based on his response, I surrendered to the procedure without a sedative of any sort.

Donned in my hospital gown, I laid on my left side on the examination table. I did not see the size of the needle he was going to use for the biopsy, but I certainly felt it. I could feel his hands shaking, and the shot itself was of course painful. "Wow," he exclaimed. "I have never felt such hard bone before. I will be surprised if there is anything wrong with your bone." He claimed that he had to repeat this torture because he did not draw enough fluid initially. I cannot describe the excruciating pain this caused.

The days that followed were miserable. I got up, got dressed, and drove back to work. I should have switched doctors after the first treatment, but I was willing to go back to him. I did not hold his actions personally against him. I knew that I could not cope with the pain on my own, but, with the grace of God, I did endure it.

I thank God, who knows, hears, and sees what we can never know. He saw that this was a spiritual warfare and that this battle was the Lord's. No wonder why I seemed rather indifferent, because God totally made it impossible for me to react to or to take charge of my own insufficiency. Thank you, Jesus.

Academically there are required courses to complete successfully before we can move from one grade to another. The courses must be studied, and acceptable grades must be earned before graduation. Well, divine testing is similar. If you want to advance, you must be willing to submit, surrender, and let God (the potter and designer) mold you into the vessel fit for his use. We are the clay.

I was given an appointment to return within one week. By that time, the test results would be back. The doctor did not call me; therefore, I expected to receive positive news. Oh, was I fooled. The doctor walked in with another person, who later introduced himself as a doctor as well. The diagnosis soon followed. I would never have dreamt of such a result—not because

Mercy Beyond Measure

I thought I was too good, but because it just had not crossed my mind.

I thank God, however, for being with me through it all. God has brought me to know Him, and whatever happens will be to his glory and exaltation. It is this life-transforming experience that I am about to share with you. This was an unplanned journey with an unknown destination and outcome. God brought me out in triumph and victory. Jesus, Son of the Most High God, delivered and set me free and placed me on a solid foundation.

March 8, 1995, was the month and day on which I was going to either trust my Lord and Savior Jesus Christ or believe a lie and allow the devil to feast and feed on me—my body, soul, and mind. I had been a healthy, active individual with only three prior hospitalizations—from childbirths and malaria.

The news was handed to me: I had cancer, multiple myeloma. It seemed as if my life had shattered into pieces. I can only liken it to a custom in my culture, in which children look forward to their first trip to the stream to fetch water for their mother with their new clay pot—one that a mother purchases for her child for this first important stage of the child's maturity. Now imagine that a young girl fetches the water, carries the clay pot on her head, and begins her walk home. Just as she is a few yards away from her house, where her mom is waiting for her, she trips on something. There goes her clay pot and its contents, with one thunderous bang. Her mother runs to her daughter and holds her,

Mercy Beyond Measure

wiping the young girl's tears, telling her that it is all right, and promising to buy her another pot.

I actually heard a bang too, as if the clay pot that was my life had shattered in pieces. Yet my sweet and wonderful mother wasn't there to hold me and reassure me that it was going to be all right. God was with me, however, and only God could piece it back together, and he has. To God be the glory!

The doctor then went on to discuss the options that were available in treating such a form of cancer. He strongly urged me to consider receiving a bone-marrow transplant, adding that if I were his wife or sister, he would recommend such treatment. He thought that given my age and strength, I would survive it. He said I would undergo high doses of chemotherapy and radiation, and then my blood would be given back to me after they had screened it thoroughly.

I asked my doctor how he would know that all the cancer cells had been removed. He conceded that neither he nor any other doctor could guarantee that all the bad cells would be removed. I asked him what the life expectancy was for someone who receives a bone-marrow transplant. He said it was about three to five years, and sometimes longer.

On that day, I became a cancer patient. I ceased to be that healthy and vibrant young lady; mother of two wonderful sons; wife; and daughter. I became a hostage determined to escape. I became a soldier sworn to victory in the name of Jesus Christ. *Multiple myeloma* was attached to my name, a diagnosis that came with

Mercy Beyond Measure

a vengeance to consume me in two or three months, according to the oncologist.

It is this story that I'm going to tell you. It is also a story about God's tender love and compassion, and his oath to allow us not to drown or be burned. Come with me to be encouraged and revived in God's faithfulness.

I told my doctor that I had absorbed all of what he had said to me but that I wanted him to know that I had a Father who could heal me. "Who is that?" asked the doctor. I responded, "Jesus." My doctor chuckled kindly and said, "It is Jesus who has put me here to help you."

He went on to tell the story of a man who climbed on a rooftop during a flood, believing that Jesus would rescue him. The man refused to be rescued when a boat—and later a helicopter—arrived to retrieve him. The floodwaters eventually rose and consumed him, leading to his death. The man went to heaven and asked God why He did not come to rescue him. God responded, "I did send you a boat and a plane, but you refused them both."

The doctor ended by telling me to consider what he had said and to tell my husband to come with me. I asked the doctor what would happen should I choose nothing, to which he responded, "We are talking two to three months, and you will be gone."

Reality set in. I felt as if I had been hit with a ton of bricks. With my head tossed backward, my tears began to flow. The doctor handed me some Kleenex and reached out his hand toward mine. As the tears fell, I shook my head in disbelief. Breathing became laborious, and comforting was needed.

Mercy Beyond Measure

The Holy Spirit came and wiped away my tears and restored my thoughts as I thanked the doctor and left. The next appointment was just one week away; my life from that point had changed forever. The Holy Spirit spoke softly to me, advising that I should treat this as a mere detour or disruption. Driving back to work, I began to reflect on what the doctor had just said, but I was not heavily weighed down. This was divine favor.

Second Opinion

Something strange happened during the first night following the diagnosis. I had severe chest pain that made breathing, movement, and so forth extremely unbearable. The only tolerable position was sitting up straight. This pain continued for three days, making me lose my appetite. By the next appointment date, my weight had dropped.

The doctor explained every detail of the option of having a bone-marrow transplant, which would involve receiving very high doses of chemotherapy. The severe chest pain, which held me hostage for three days, did not seem important to the doctor. He simply said, "Hmm, I have never heard of that before. Frankly, it does not have anything to do with the disease."

Mercy Beyond Measure

He emphasized that there was a very good chance that I would lead a normal and productive life afterward, despite being told earlier that my life expectancy would be between three and five years. No man knows the truth except God; in God we trust. It is only God who directs man in all knowledge and understanding.

My husband absorbed all that he could, and we went home. At my next appointment, the doctor was about to schedule me for a bone-marrow procedure before our leaving his office, but I discouraged him. His speed was suspicious to me. I had to seek divine guidance. Divine wisdom and guidance were crucial in every facet of this battle. There was something unsettling about this oncologist. Something was not right.

My suspicions deepened when he jokingly said, "I will give you an order for a wig if you are concerned about losing your hair. I see you have very good hair." In addition, no other treatment mattered to him except the aggressive bone-marrow transplant with high doses of chemotherapy. Thank God, who puts people in our paths, because the name of a doctor whom my husband and I had met in the past came to mind right away. We went to see him immediately. It was he who referred us to a renowned oncologist.

A second opinion was sought from one of the best cancer experts in New England, and treatment options were discussed during this time. This doctor took the time to discuss and answer all the amateur questions we posed to him. He called the oncologist to discuss treatment options other than the bone-marrow transplant. He realized that such a procedure would be too much for anyone to handle. The doctor must have spent almost two hours with us. The concern and caring expression on his countenance would not go unnoticed. What a great person. God bless him.

We left his office wondering how much we had to pay him. However, Jesus Christ, who is the author and finisher of my life, stepped in once again. At the desk, we learned that the doctor had instructed them not to charge us for the visit. What a mighty Father we have! The doctor was in a private practice, and our HMO policy would not pay for this private consultation. We did not anticipate the cost for the visit, but we stepped out on faith, believing that He who is able to do exceedingly abundantly above all that we ask or think would take care of it. He surely did. What an awesome shepherd!

"Now unto him that is able to do exceeding abundantly above all that we ask or think, according to the power that worketh in us" (Eph. 3:20).

The diagnosis came as a shock, even though God had spoken through my pastor. This monster known as cancer was the last thing on my mind, so there was never a time of preplanning as to what to do with this mountain of evil spirit. Yes, cancer is an evil spirit; it is of the devil and comes to steal, destroy, and kill. How many people, if any, know that they will be diagnosed with cancer or any other disease? It is the farthest thing on one's mind.

It was not a time to cry, although that took place at the initial announcement by the oncologist. My husband took a stand and summed it up by saying, "Don't even think you

Mercy Beyond Measure

have any shoulder to cry on. We are going to face this thing with clear eyes." The Lord had prepared me for the ordeal to come.

The next appointment came around rather quickly, and my husband and I realized that we had not discussed what we would say to the doctor regarding treatment choice. When the doctor came in and asked us what our decision was regarding the bone-marrow transplant, we both shrugged our shoulders. The doctor advised us that we needed to hurry on a decision because we did not really have much time.

During a second consultation, with a different doctor, we were told about some new chemo tablets, which were thought to work well with me. What a coincidence that was! Right after the diagnosis and the doctor's recommendation for a bone-marrow transplant with high doses of chemotherapy treatment, the news was flooded with bad reports on cancer. A well-known anchorwoman died of chemotherapy overdose at one of the best cancer treatment centers in the country. Another death occurred from an incorrect prescription.

With all the negative news, divine inspired stillness was needed. This would echo from within: "I do not need a write-up in the *Wall Street Journal* in order for me to heed or adhere to divine intervention or warning." Another appointment was set up, and more tests were sent to the lab.

At least three out of seven days, the evening news (either local or national) is not over without something being mentioned about cancer: impending research, death, medication, and so forth. Either verbally or nonverbally, some people

Mercy Beyond Measure

deny that such a diagnosis will ever be given to them or to someone they know. But what happens when cancer is at your door? You never knew or thought it would be you, and you were not sickly before. Every day someone is being given very little hope. They are sent home to go and die or to set their affairs in order. Even when medical interventions are suggested, hope for a positive future often remains bleak.

There is hope, however, in God and his Son, Jesus. Whose report would you believe? Well, this is what befell me in 1995. Even with the limited suggestions that the doctor presented, there wasn't much of a long-term chance, from man's perspective. Imagine being told, "I'm sorry, but there is not much I can do for you. You might live three to five years if you choose to have surgery." If you have spent all your savings and have exhausted all efforts in the natural realm with its modern technology, with no success, do not despair! Jehovah-rapha has the answer. It is Him who has the final say, not man!

Our Father in heaven and all His promises have not changed. Turn to God. Become violent in faith. Begin the journey to touch the helm of His garment and make the way to receive your healing, because the Word of God states, "For I am the LORD that healeth thee" (Exod. 15:26). God does not lie; trust and believe God's report. Implore God for the Holy Spirit for direction and instructions. God being the same yesterday, today, and forever, He will surely hear your petition and pleas. "Ask, and it shall be given you; seek, and ye shall find; knock, and it shall be opened unto you: For everyone that asketh receiveth; and he that seeketh findeth; and to him that knocketh it shall be opened" (Matt. 7:7-8).

He promised He would bring me out. I believed Him, and I studied the Word with intensity and curiosity. The more I read the Word, the more peace came upon me. I became deeply engrossed because of the stillness and soothing sweetness I derived from the Word. What did I do? I cried unto the Lord, and He heard me; I called unto His holy name, and He answered my pleas. He answered prayers yesterday. He is answering prayers today. He will answer prayers forever. Trust in God and his promises. All God wants is a believing and trusting childlike heart.

Mercy Akpan

Resisting the Devil

My body became a combat zone as every imaginable pain of this world started attacking me. My pastor was out of the state at the time, so I could not call him. I was unemployed; shortly before the diagnosis, I had resigned from my job in order to start a business. That venture was still in the introductory stage, which meant that all my savings and resources had been channeled into starting the business. My life-insurance policy was canceled because I was no longer employed.

My family was a major concern to me; I pondered how they would fare without me. As I was slowly dwelling on this thought, a church member stopped by, and we decided to go to the grocery store. After I had finished shopping, I

Mercy Beyond Measure

told her I would be waiting for her in the car. A few minutes later, she came out to tell me that she had seen our church deacon and his wife in the store and that she had briefly mentioned my diagnosis to them.

Within a few minutes, I was sharing the details of my situation to the other three. The deacon prayed for me, which released some of the burden and mental anguish, and gave me some Scriptures to read (Matthew chapters 8 and 9, which detail the miraculous works of Jesus). The deacon told me to focus all my attention on God and to believe that He is able to heal. He also said that he would mention my diagnosis to my pastor, as the pastor would be calling him sometime that evening. When I returned home, I engrossed myself in the two recommended chapters, which were packed with God's sovereignty, grace, and faithfulness.

Pastor Edred A. Black returned on the scheduled date and immediately set up an appointment to see me, despite his hectic schedule. He prayed for me and anointed me with holy oil, and he cautioned me to hold on to the prophecy that God gave through him concerning the situation. He prayed and reassured me of God's promise to deliver me. His prayer and encouragement strengthened me.

The chest pain started subsiding, but the pain in my right arm worsened. I was unable to do much of anything that required the use of my right hand. I am very right-handed, so you can imagine the difficulty. Bathing, cooking, styling my hair, brushing my teeth, and even cleansing my face became a chore and burdensome.

Mercy Beyond Measure

The climax of my frustration was in church; it was painful to clap. The pain was so terrible, and mentally I should have given up clapping to my Lord and Savior. Spiritually, however, I knew that each painful clap was leading to relief and healing.

Sure enough, I remained standing and clapping, and with each stabbing pain, I said, "By [His] stripes [I am] healed" (1 Pet. 2:24). The pain would immediately cease from that area and would travel or move to a different area (from shoulder to elbow, to palm or fingers) until it would eventually cease. Glory to God! Even this temporary relief was much appreciated and needed.

In our Father's house, where there is praise and worship, healing and other deliverances take place. You see, God is an awesome God. I believe that there is nothing that we encounter in this world that God has not prepared or warned us about before its manifestation. Go to church, and be involved, because you never know when God is going to speak to you through a pastor.

The following week, I decided to stay home from work on a Monday. Our youngest son also had a day off from school. Both of us were sitting down in the living room, when I got up to get something from my bedroom. That was when I first smelled the foul odor. I was fear-stricken, and the Holy Spirit led me to discern that this was a spirit of death. I immediately turned and dashed out of the bedroom. My son then said, "Mom, do you smell something bad?" I admitted to him that I did smell it, and I told him to forget about it, but I was concerned.

Mercy Beyond Measure

By this time, the odor had permeated everywhere. It was time to fight. "And from the days of John the Baptist until now; the kingdom of heaven suffereth violence, and the violent take it by force" (Matt. 11:12). Thank you, Holy Spirit!

I got up and walked boldly into my bedroom to get the holy oil, and I became violent in prayer. As I was praying, the odor kept getting stronger. I persisted in prayer throughout every room and every closet, binding the spirit of death in Jesus' name. I called upon the Blood of Jesus until the Lord finally drove that spirit out. The Holy Spirit had directed me to open the door to let it outside and to bind it to never come back, and so I did as he commanded me. The devil cannot stand the Blood of Jesus; it paralyzes the devil. It causes demons to freeze. "And when I see the blood, I will pass over you, and the plague shall not be upon you to destroy you" (Exod. 12:13).

The physical and mental pain was indescribable before and after visits to the doctor. It became so intense that my husband and I decided it was best to keep appointment dates to ourselves. I would show him the appointment slip without reading the date out loud, because I was too sick either a day or two before the appointment. This worked, but then it took a different turn. We did not announce the date prior to going to see the doctor; therefore, I got very ill after such visits (usually the next day). I told the doctor that I might be allergic to the building, but he said that did not have anything to do with it. Keeping appointments was not easy. I was reluctant.

Mercy Beyond Measure

Following church one Sunday afternoon, while just resting in bed, the name of a lady whom I had met approximately ten years earlier echoed through my mind. She'd been in my life when my youngest son suffered from severe asthma. At that time, no medications, inhalers, or nebulizers could ease his suffering—that was, until a friend told me about a lady who was a clinical nutritionist.

Ten years later, that same name flashed across my bedroom wall. I heard, "Call her, and she will tell you what to do." I quickly got out of bed and started looking for her number. I felt a surge of peace within me. Her home telephone number was unpublished, but I managed to locate her business number and called her the next day.

We had a phone consultation, and then she immediately instructed me to eliminate certain foods from my diet. She informed me of what supplements to take, and easy exercises to do regularly. You see, it pays to listen and be still, because He who knows us before He sent us to this world also tells us what to do for His living temple of which we are. If we believe in God the Creator, we must believe in Christ the Healer. At least five times, the Holy Spirit had told me to take care of my body. Therefore, after the woman completed the consultation and promised to ship the supplements to me, there was no question in my mind that God was real and alive and that He was going to bring me out as He had revealed through my pastor.

Within a few days, the shipment arrived. I started a fresh eating habit and took the supplements. I resorted to most of my ancestral foods, vegetables, and plenty of water. I remained prayerful and in daily Bible study, in addition to fasting occasionally and attending church regularly.

The six-week visit came. After looking at the results of my blood work, my doctor said, "Hmm, if it ain't broke, don't fix it." Hallelujah! I am telling you that God is good and that Jesus is alive. Jesus is the same yesterday, today, and forever. The doctor also added that I looked good. I believe that it was not the supplements that led to such a positive report; it was simply God's grace and compassion, and also the fervent prayer of the righteous, which availeth much.

My church and family prayed. "Is any sick among you? Let him call for the elders of the church; and let them pray over him, anointing him with oil in the name of the Lord: And the prayer of faith shall save the sick, and the Lord shall raise him up; and if he have committed sins, they shall be forgiven him" (James 5:14-15).

It was a relief to know that I would not have to return to that facility. Prior to the doctor uttering what he said, I had prayed to God to keep me from that building. I made up my mind to abandon completely my whole being to Jesus, Son of the living God. I said, "Lord, you created me. Therefore, no one knows my body like you do. If I am to be healed, it is you alone who can do it."

Guess what happened that evening? I started hurting all over again. Every symptom and feeling resurfaced, including some very strange ones. Satan is the author of confusion and chaos, and he hates to see God's children get healed and delivered, so he struck again at me. I became so sick from that moment forward. However, I was determined not to allow unbelief—which, to me, is a sin because it undermines the sovereignty of the Lord, my God. This was very scary to me. Trusting God was crucial no matter what the body was saying or feeling.

Mercy Akpan

Divine Prescription

About nine months ago, I was awakened in a dream and was told to start taking willow and kasper. I was told that I could even give it to my children if they had a headache. The moment that I was informed of this, I could not sleep. I sat up, fully awake and alert until sunrise.

In the morning, I called up the health-food store. Never before had I heard of these two things. The manager confirmed that there was something called *willow*. The store manager read its uses to me, and I learned that it was helpful in many cancer cases. *Kasper* was difficult, as the manager did not know what it was.

But guess what? One morning I was listening to a Christian radio-station program called *Here's to Your Health*. The guest speaker was a

Mercy Beyond Measure

gentleman from the Swedish Herbal Institute. He gave the telephone number over the air for callers to order some of their products, and so I wrote it down and decided to call right after the program. I spoke with a very nice young lady and asked her about kasper. She did not know about the particular herb but promised to contact a friend of hers who was very knowledgeable about the subject.

I stand in awe at the ways in which God fulfills his purpose and plans. One week later, the young lady's friend told me that what I was referring to as *kasper* was the same as *capsicum*, and she gave me the telephone number for a company that manufactured the herb. I spell *kasper* with a *k* because of how it sounded when the name was revealed to me. With a little more research, I learned that cayenne pepper (red pepper) was another form of capsicum. So I started adding a little cayenne to my diet, and I felt good.

I also did some research on willow and learned more about its usefulness in many cancer cases. It comes in either capsule form or tree-bark form for tea. In the dream I was told to drink it; therefore, I decided to order the bark form. I steeped it and drank it cold or hot. At the same time, I decided to experiment with it, by applying it to a growth that was on my finger at that time. It worked: The growth was healed! What a mighty God we serve!

I did not experience any pain when I incorporated willow into my diet, but then the devil began playing games with me. I did not feel like drinking the tea any longer. I could not explain why, but I was no longer motivated, so I fell to that temptation. However, it was not long before I started drinking the tea again. You see, God knows us because He created us. He knows our strengths and weaknesses and also knows how to motivate us and get us back on course.

The devil could not get me to subject myself to surgery and chemotherapy, so it attempted to attack my immune system. My entire body felt as if it had shut down, like a zombie: no appetite, just slow deterioration. Then another divine visitation occurred. I was told to eat something with the hottest pepper I could possibly stand. That did it, and I became alive.

Other Attacks

The next attack was serious constipation. Another divine intervention occurred, in which I was told that adding charcoal to my diet would alleviate this problem. Believe me, I never knew that charcoal could be taken internally.

I shared this revelation with my husband, who responded, "Oh no! You will not take that one. We are not going to do that, because some of these things could come from the devil as well. I have never heard of anyone taking charcoal." I was convinced this was given to me divinely, because I had committed this whole situation to God, and He is faithful. I started taking charcoal capsules, and I felt healthy and energized again—and my blood work remained good. What an awesome God!

Mercy Beyond Measure

There's no telling what would have happened but for this divine intervention. However, please do not go out and purchase these things. I do not endorse their use, nor am I telling you that these things will heal you. I am merely sharing with you that if you trust and believe in God, our heavenly Father the Holy Creator, and his Son, Jesus, you can ask anything in his name and He will grant it.

A week later, things changed. That morning, I followed my usual routine: showered, dressed, and drove to work. Around eleven, however, I started having difficulty breathing, followed by dizziness and fainting spells. I managed to call an ambulance and was rushed to the hospital. I felt as if I were going to die; both legs were numb, and the nurse could not find my vein to initiate an intravenous drip or to draw some blood. The numbness seemed to travel upward toward my upper-body chamber.

I quietly recited Psalm 23 in my hospital bed. Shortly thereafter, two fellow church members who had been notified about my situation stood beside me, and we prayed together. Our prayers were heard. The Master did it again—to God be the glory. They could not find anything wrong with me, and I was sent home. I felt as if I had been beaten, thrashed, and deprived of sleep for days; even so, I was unable to sleep. Only Jesus, the Christ, knew what had happened to me and brought me out of it.

Following the emergency-room episode, I no longer experienced severe pain in my arm. However, every night between 9:00 and 9:45, I became light-headed; breathing was laborious; my feet were ice-cold; my heart raced rapidly;

Mercy Beyond Measure

and I became totally helpless and lethargic. I would put on socks one minute, only to have them off the next minute.

The doctors kept saying that I was experiencing anxiety attacks. They'd ask if I were anxious about anything, and I would say no, so there was really nothing they could do for me. Therefore, going to the emergency room was no longer an option. Day after day, my family members took care of me by elevating my legs, lowering my head, packing cold washcloths on my forehead, and praying.

Driving became a chore because my attacks would occur at traffic lights. (God is good.) Imagine if these attacks affected me while the car was in motion. His grace is sufficient for us! Throughout these attacks, I kept applying the Blood of Jesus and claiming healing. The Bible became a daily comfort and companion. I meditated on these Scriptures:

> But he was wounded for our transgressions, he was bruised for our iniquities: the chastisement of our peace was upon him; and with His stripes we are healed. (Isa. 53:5)

> My grace is sufficient for thee: for my strength is made perfect in weakness. (2 Cor. 12:9)

His Personal Appearance

In October 1996, something strange happened to me. I was scheduled to travel to Africa on October 9 for a very important event. In the beginning of the month, however, I was deadly ill and helpless, although totally unrelated to what the doctor had diagnosed. My head felt like it was in a barrel, while my body was weak and limp. I could not eat, drink, bathe, or dress myself. I was so sick that my children were trying to give me orange juice, because I could not eat. I was flat on my back, unable to speak, and my doctor had said that there was nothing wrong with me!

The devil has the power of destructive cleverness. It would say, "It is destined all will die. This is your time. Accept it and go on.

Sooner or later, others will go." It took another twist as well: "Do you want to be a burden to your children? Why do you even want to hang around? There is nothing to dying...Just accept it as being your own turn."

From a natural man's perspective, I allowed myself to observe the circumstances around me, instead of rising above sight and operating in faith that God, who raised up Jesus from the dead, was able to heal me and make me whole to make the trip. God had his plan, and his plan is always best for us.

> For my thoughts are not your thoughts, neither are your ways my ways, saith the LORD. For as the heavens are higher than the earth, so are my ways higher than your ways, and my thoughts than your

Mercy Beyond Measure

thoughts. For as the rain cometh down, and the snow from heaven, and returneth not thither, but watereth the earth, and maketh it bring forth and bud, that it may give seed to the sower, and bread to the eater: So shall my word be that goeth forth out of my mouth: it shall not return unto me void, but it shall accomplish that which I please, and it shall prosper in the thing whereto I sent it. For ye shall go out with joy, and be led forth with peace: the mountains and the hills shall break forth before you into singing, and all the trees of the field shall clap their hands. (Isa. 55:8-12)

A vision came to me while I was on my back, in bed, propped up, and trying to figure out what was wrong—while, at the same time, praying within my heart for God's touch and healing. I was so concerned about my children. I thought about the young man, the only son of his mother, whom Jesus raised to life and handed him back to his mother who was a widow (Luke 7:11-15). The mother's cries moved Jesus; therefore, I petitioned that God would do the same for my children's sake.

I remember dozing off and He answering me in the form of this vision: I saw two arms on a tall man's frame, with the most delicate white garment embroidered with eyelets and sleeves dangling down. His arms and hands were stretched out, and He encircled my upper chamber with his arms and hands, using the garment to wrap me with just my face exposed. He said to me, "Look, this is how I am going to

Mercy Beyond Measure

take you to Nigeria and back." We walked, He supporting me as I rested against him. His outstretched arms and hands were pointed toward my bedroom door.

When I woke, I was overwhelmed with what had happened. I started crying because of joy and his grace. I did not see his face. I did see, however, his outstretched arms and hands, his delicate, white, embroidered garment with large sleeves that dangled even after He wrapped his arms around me.

I sat up and started speaking. I went to the bathroom and showered. I told my husband what had happened. I believed what I saw, and I knew that God had taken care of that sickness, whatever it was. However, my husband insisted on our going to the clinic. He wasn't convinced that I would no longer be ill during the night, as had been the case for some time.

Tests were done, and the doctor came back to say, "I do not really see anything wrong with her. To be perfectly honest with you, with this type of lab report of her blood, I doubt very much if she has what they say she has. The symptoms that you described to me are global, pointing to nothing of significance. She can travel anywhere she desires."

I looked at my husband and said, "I told you what the Holy Spirit said to me." His response was, "I'm not taking any more chances. I wanted someone to take a look at you instead of trying to diagnose you over the phone." No one can treat you like Jesus! We returned home, and I was able to pack for my trip.

Mercy Beyond Measure

The following day was Sunday. At church, my pastor took me by my hand and led me to the altar. He prayed for me, although totally unaware of what I had been through. God spoke to him. What a difference the anointing makes! I was gone for four weeks in Nigeria, and the Lord protected and brought me back as He had promised. Hallelujah!

Mercy Akpan

Obedience Is Better Than Sacrifice

In 1997, we moved to be near our youngest son's school. Before we started packing, I had a clear order from the Holy Spirit to leave behind our bedroom set. Not quite understanding this instruction, I prayed for clarification and was told that I could give it away or do whatever I wanted with it but that I could not bring it with us.

At the time, we did not plan on replacing the bedroom set. What we had was still in very good condition. The instruction was to sleep on the floor for six months and occasionally sleep on the sofa. How was I going to tell my husband? It was tough, but I knew I had to obey. When I finally did tell my husband, he asked me if we could at least take the dresser. "No," I replied.

"We are told not to take any of the bedroom furniture."

To my surprise, he calmly went along with this order—without his usual reasoning—and we moved without taking any bedroom furniture. We moved into the new place and slept on the floor using spreads, quilts, and blankets, while occasionally sleeping on the sofa. There was no complaint from either of us.

We were to spend at least six months in that sleeping arrangement, as the order was. After only two months, however, I made the mistake of mentioning this divine mandate to a friend. The next thing I knew, she told her friend, who immediately offered to bring by a queen-size bed for us. I turned down the offer immediately, and thank God that I did.

I learned something from that experience: Keep whatever the Lord gives to you to yourself. Do not rush to tell friends or people. Learn from the Blessed Virgin Mary. "But Mary kept all these things, and pondered them in her heart" (Luke 2:19). Do not run to tell of your revelations unless you are mandated to do so. When I was growing up, my father always told us to be swift to hear but slow to speak. This has remained with me, but I almost blew it out of ignorance. Thank God for the Holy Spirit, who guides us and brings those things to memory. Money cannot equate the value of the revelations that God gave me during that time. Intimacy and fellowship with God are beautiful and valuable.

> But God hath chosen the foolish things of the world to confound the wise; and God

hath chosen the weak things of the world to confound the things which are mighty; And base things of the world, and things which are despised, hath God chosen, yea, and things which are not, to bring to nought things that are: That no flesh should glorify in his presence. (1 Cor. 1:27-29)

My Lord allowed me to become intimate with Him. It is good to obey God's order and adhere to his voice. Doing so lightens the darkened valleys and assures us of His abiding presence, and you know that you are surely guarded.

Looking back, if I had accepted the offer of the bed or had given in to purchasing a bedroom set, I think that I would have become a weeping philosopher for the rest of my life because my loss could never be measured. Thank God for Jesus. Obedience is better than sacrifice. "Hath the LORD as great delight in burnt offering and sacrifices, as in obeying the voice of the LORD? Behold, to obey is better than sacrifice, and to hearken than the fat of rams. For rebellion is as the sin of witchcraft, and stubbornness is as iniquity and idolatry" (1 Sam. 15:22-23). God's love prevented me from falling into the tempter's trap.

I am not blaming my friend. She meant well. But you must know where it hurts, how deep it hurts. You must also recognize that the hotter the fiery furnace, the more decorative your crown will be, and the greater the anointing will be. Hallelujah!

You also must decide how much fruit you want to yield, and you must be attentive and

Mercy Beyond Measure

sensitive to divine order and command. You must decide not to settle for a generic anointing. The deeper and peculiar your anointing, the more attentive and protective you must be of it. You are going to prove what type of soldier you are. How much can you endure without wavering while waiting for the manifestation of the promise?

My family and I went to New York to visit a very dear friend and also to do a little back-to-school shopping for our sons. The boys had never been to the city, so they were excited. The Lord took us there safely.

I can remember feeling good physically. I felt so good that I actually felt as if I were floating with such blessed assurance and fullness, with a secure feeling and attitude. My inner spirit felt peaceful and established. My girlfriend was actually teasing me that I was behaving as if I did not have a care in the world. A very unusual feeling of inner peace and security hovered over me.

We got on the train to proceed to Chinatown, and that was when Satan tried to interrupt my joy. Reaching down to grab the arm of the seat while getting on the train, I immediately heard a crack in my right upper arm, as if a piece of dried wood snapped in two. Perspiration was all over me. Glory to God, a young lady looked up at me and asked if I would like to sit down. I accepted and thanked her; to find such kindness in a busy city is rare. God bless her. I still pray for her.

The next stop was for us. We got off the train, and my family tried to make a sling to support my arm. They got ice, but the pain was so severe that despite my trying to be brave, I just could not shop. So we had to return to my friend's home in New Rochelle, and we returned to Massachusetts two days later. God is a good God; on my own, I could not have made it back in the car. Glory to God.

We immediately went to see an orthopedic surgeon, who ordered a sling and pain-relief pills and concluded that the arm was fractured as a result of the multiple myeloma. I responded, "Devil, you are a liar." He suggested that I go to an oncologist.

Due to our health insurance, this would mean my returning to the oncologist who did not want to try anything other than the bone-marrow transplant and high doses of chemotherapy. I dreaded the thought of going back to him. He had not given me any hope at all. I did not know what to do.

One thing I knew for sure was to continue in prayer, and I fasted, as the Lord gave me the direction and ability to do so. I knew that no matter what I felt like, I would be healed, because God said so through Pastor Black. He is a faithful God. During that time, I found consolation in the following Scripture: "No weapon that is formed against thee shall prosper; and every tongue that shall rise against thee in judgment thou shalt condemn" (Isa. 54:17).

I took the pain-relief pills that the orthopedic surgeon gave me, which temporarily eased the pain. As time went on, however, their relief wore off. The doctor told me that he would not renew the prescription, as he already had twice. He stressed that I must go to the oncologist, to which I reluctantly agreed to do.

I was whisked in right away. The oncologist examined me, gave me a prescription, and told me that I could be paralyzed within a very short time. He urged me to go through with the bone-marrow transplant and chemotherapy. It was the beginning of the mental warfare. I left his office feeling very burdened—until my girlfriend called. Childhood friends are true; knowing each other's strengths and weaknesses, you can bring out the best in one another.

The Call to Wake Up

Thank God for some people having the spirit of obedience. While waiting for the next appointment, a phone call came from my girlfriend Diana—who I nicknamed *Lady Di*—in Oklahoma City: "Girl, what's the matter? What's going on there?" I replied, "Nothing."

Then she said, "You better talk to me, because I am paying for this call and am not going to hang up until you tell me what is happening over there." Knowing Lady Di meant business, I had to be honest with her. I told her about the diagnosis and the treatment that the doctor had suggested.

She listened until I finished, and then she said, "Girl, what did those people do to your brain when you moved there? Where is the

Mercy Beyond Measure

person that I know? The person I am talking about is the one who would put her two hands on her hips and tell that doctor that her father taught her to fight when something was not right. She would tell that doctor that you are not going to have the bone-marrow transplant, because you are not a chicken, because all it does is kill people like chickens. Do you hear me? Where is your boldness, girl? Where is your brain? You told me about your daddy and the strength and confidence he instilled in you. If I can remember that, why can't you? You have to fight, and you will win because God is your healer."

Lady Di is married to a minister. I was fired up, and her encouragement was all I needed to stir up my faith and strength for the battle that was before me. When faced with situations, it's often difficult to reason, and it takes someone from the outside to motivate us. Her prayers and long-distance phone calls were innumerable. I thank God through Jesus for her.

During that time, Satan used every tactic to persuade me to succumb to its traps and schemes. I knew that the moment I caved in, I would have fully endorsed the devil. What do I mean? When the doctor told me that I had two or three months to live, it was a shock—to put it mildly. I had a lot of plans to pursue, plans typical of a young lady with young sons. Death was the least of my concerns. I had dreams, visions, and goals to achieve. I wanted to fly as high as possible.

Without life insurance, I was faced with wondering which insurance company would touch me. People told me I shouldn't even try, because they would turn me down. Desperate and not being fully rooted in the Word, I made a few calls and was scheduled for a physical. The agent came out, all forms and applications were filed, and I was accepted for term life coverage; for fifteen years, the premium would be taken directly from my bank account.

I struggled to pay the monthly premiums. It was an added stress that I brought upon myself. Many months went by, until it got to the point where I couldn't afford the premiums anymore, and so the policy was canceled. It was actually quite a relief. Throughout the period that the policy was in effect, Satan tried his hardest to persuade me to accept a death verdict. Two years' worth of premiums went down the drain.

A particular Christian radio station became my daily companion during that time. It was on the station that I heard of a doctor who practiced alternative medicine in Florida. Impressed by what I heard, I called his office for an appointment. I was most impressed by the mere fact that he said he did not believe in chemotherapy and radiation. In September my husband took me to Florida to see this doctor. I also knew that the overall healing would come from our God, who created us.

The doctor did not accept insurance. Everything was on a cash basis and payable upon completion of each visit. The doctor ordered a complete physical and blood work. I had never had such detailed, thorough laboratory work done before—even my hair samples were taken and tested. I was given an appointment to return for the treatment. I would have to take intravenous infusions, which the

Mercy Beyond Measure

doctor would mix himself, and he supposedly did so better than any other doctor in the United States. He could not tell us exactly how many infusions I would need; it would depend on how I responded to each of them. His ballpark estimate was that I would need anywhere from one to thirty. Each infusion cost $73.

I returned home and continued praying and studying the Word. Remember, my right arm was still in a sling; therefore, I could not use my right hand. Eating, writing, dressing, bathing, and driving were nearly impossible. I had to learn to feed myself with my left hand. I even tried to write with my left hand, which wasn't easy.

We all know that the devil remains busy and is a master of chaos, and I guess it wasn't satisfied yet. Soon after my life insurance policy was canceled, another dart was fired at me. I had a slight cold and was coughing quite frequently. My back started hurting badly one morning, shooting me with intense pain. Looking for relief, I took some of the pain medication that the doctor had given me for my right arm. My movement became impaired, and getting in and out of my bed became a chore as well as a nightmare. I did not know what was happening to me. I could not even go to church.

The pain was awful—only God alone knows, as He was the only one who kept me and saw me through it all. I prayed to God to help me so I would not become incontinent, and I restricted my fluid intake. Thank God for being such a prayer-answering God and protective Father; I never did have trouble with incontinence—that would have broken me mentally. Thank God that Jesus knows what we will never know. God's strength is made perfect in our weakness. Our heavenly Father knows his children, how each of us is. Thank God for Jesus, for his continuous intercession. Thank God for his compassion. Oh, how He takes care of us!

The back pain coupled with the pain of my right arm started to wear me down. I did not know what to do. My husband suggested we go back to see the doctor who had not given us much hope, because no other doctor would touch me unless they got in touch with my original doctor—due to the type of health insurance we had at the time. The family discussed it, and we agreed to go back.

I was told that I could end up crippled and in a wheelchair because of my back and hip pain. He was adamant that I should go in for a bone-marrow transplant. We left his office that day drained and exhausted. A very hopeless picture had been painted. But we knew "from whence cometh my help" (Ps. 121:1).

Healing through the Stripes of Jesus!

No pain medication could offer relief, yet I could not bear the pain; it was adamant and unrelenting. I could not lie down or stand up. I tried to walk around, but this was not possible. I was alone, all alone. There was no apparent physical body present with me.

Then something strange happened to me. I became disoriented, and words began to echo in my subconscious: "The thirty-nine stripes I took was for a time like this. In those thirty-nine stripes, one of them was for cancer, and another for AIDS. Every disease and sickness was in those stripes." The next thing I recall, I woke to find myself in a supine position—and the pain completely gone.

Mercy Akpan

On November 17, my husband and I returned to Florida. We arrived safely, by God's grace, and went directly to the doctor's office. During the consultation, I told him that the doctor in Massachusetts had suggested radiation to me but that I had declined it. This same doctor, who told my husband and I in July (just months prior) that he did not believe in radiation and chemotherapy, told us that I should have taken it and that he was not opposed to it!

To ease some of my pain—and believe me, walking at this point was totally by divine grace—the doctor ordered acupuncture treatment, but this was to no avail. The acupuncturist was a Christian and said she would pray for me that night during her devotional time.

Mercy Beyond Measure

The next day, I took the infusion as scheduled. My Lord, I could hardly move around. Walking was unbearable, and I knew that the Almighty was the one carrying me. I am sure I was borne on eagles' wings.

After I had received the infusion, the doctor sent me to another doctor for an X ray. I overheard the doctor's phone call, urging the radiologist to stay open until I got there. The doctor emphasized, "You must see her today." God directed my husband there, and the doctor waited for us. (Thank God for having blessed us with a rental car, as opposed to having to hire a taxi like we did on our first visit.) There were no other patients. It was the radiologist, his secretary, my husband, and I. God knew how much pain I was experiencing and how much time it would take to get me on the X-ray table. It was a nightmare, and I know that I did not do it on my own. It took me forty-five minutes to get on the table, and about one hour to get up from the table after the last X ray; that was how painful it was.

Through it all, however, God touched the doctor with patience. He was very gentle and kind to me. After the reading of the X ray, he said, "You are really in pain. It is not a put-on, young lady. You have a fracture of L1-L5, plus 30 percent of your spine has collapsed. I cannot understand why you are walking, with what is going on down there. You are doing well, considering."

I managed to get back in the car, and my husband drove back to the doctor's office to take the X-ray film to him, per his order. He had told us he had to see it that day in order to know what treatment plan to follow next. My mobility was deteriorating rapidly on a daily basis. My infusion appointment was usually around 9:30 A.M. It was less than ten minutes' traveling time between Homestead, where we lodged, and the treatment center. Even so, we would have to get up around 6:00 A.M., because it took me at least one or two hours to sit up.

The pain was severe. I was even scared to drink liquid, for fear of having to get up. I am convinced that I am not the one who bore that pain, because it was just too much for a 5-foot, 120-pound body frame. It was only possible by divine intervention. Jesus bore my pain. Like Shadrach, Meshach, and Abednego, God came down to succor me in this fiery furnace. Some fires are hotter than others, and it takes God's personal appearance to bring us out. My husband would place ice packs on my back at nighttime. As the ice melted, he would offer to remove the packs, but movement was torturous and unbearable. Once in bed, I did not budge until morning; that was how severe the pain was. The infusions did not offer any relief.

On December 3, 1997, the doctor met with us in his office—a $90 visit that lasted thirty minutes—to tell my husband this: "If I were you, I would take the next available plane home." I imagine he could have told us this in the hallway, but he would have lost out on the $90 charge. But do you know what? Neither my husband nor I said a word there or after. We both merely turned and looked at one another. The devil had lost the battle on Calvary and was losing another battle as well.

Mercy Beyond Measure

Jesus, Son of the living God, gave us victory over cancer and paralysis on Calvary and through his resurrection. I meditated on all his healing and miracles, and I knew that God would not fail me; He had promised to heal me. He is a covenant keeper and a faithful Father. God strengthened us to trust and believe in him by sending his beloved Son Jesus to die for us so that we would have eternal life.

We were late getting to the airport, because my husband went to return the rental car after he had dropped me off at the main entrance. He did not want anyone else driving me, because every bump meant added pain. We were cutting it close. Guess what? Are you ready for this? When we arrived at the boarding gate, we were told that the plane was delayed, for what reason they were not quite sure. Hallelujah! We were told that they would inform us when to board and that they would allow me to board first and be comfortably seated before the other passengers. Wow! Jesus is Lord! God's grace and mercies are infinite!

We arrived safely back in Massachusetts the following Monday and went to the hospital. Instead of receiving the markings for radiation, however, I was admitted. Not only that, I also had a new doctor (oncologist), per the goodness of the sweet radiologist whom we had seen previously and felt very comfortable with.

The radiologist had concluded talking with me and started to walk out of the room when she turned back suddenly to ask me if I was satisfied with my oncologist. Hearing my response, she said she'd make arrangements for me to see a different doctor. I asked my husband to go and tell her that I'd stay with the oncologist I had before, but before I could change my mind again—as the devil came with its game-playing, telling me that I was causing trouble by getting a new oncologist—she said it was too late to change, because she had already set up everything with the new one. To God be all the glory! He rains down favors on his own.

I could not have asked for a better oncologist. When it became apparent that I had to undergo conventional cancer treatment, I had prayed to God to direct my doctor and to write my treatment plan—and that prayer was answered in this new oncologist. God will send someone to speak for you. On my own, I could not have asked for a new oncologist.

A hospital room was then assigned to me. I could not get in bed, and I did not allow anyone to help me; the pain was unbearable. I was medicated, and they allowed me to sit until the medication took effect. Four nurses assisted me into bed. God bless them.

I was to remain in bed from that point on, to be transferred only on a stretcher and only when being taken to treatments or appointments. I learned to use a bedpan, as I could not convince them to allow me to get up to use the bathroom. I felt psychologically helpless.

I saw my new doctor the next day and immediately felt as if I had known her for years. She was a beautiful, calm, and gentle lady. She spoke softly and reassuringly, letting me know what she was going to do. I told her that I had prayed to God to send me a doctor who would obey His instructions concerning me and that I trusted her to treat me as an individual, not as a statistic. She said she would do her best to not disappoint me. She was the type of doctor everyone should have: caring, kind, gentle, intelligent, and humble. I have observed her at work with other patients; she treats all her patients with love, respect, and dignity. Dr. Seetharaman, you are the best! I thank God for you.

I remember the sense of peace and security that came over me when I saw her. God was in charge of everything concerning me. I had to go through every phase of the fire, but God gave me peace. The Holy Spirit spoke to me: "Can a father ignore his child upon hearing that the child is sick? Does he not seek out the best medical care for that child?" I was convinced that my heavenly Father had everything perfectly in place.

Throughout my stay at the hospital, we prayed. Each day, my husband and our sons would join hands and pray, kissing me before they'd leave. Glory to God. Everything was peaceful, and the presence of the Holy Ghost in the room was unquestionable. My pastor and his wife came, as did some of my church members, and none of them left without praying. Prayer changes things, by changing you for things. Hallelujah!

I spent Christmas and New Year's Eve in the hospital. I did not receive a bone-marrow transplant or surgery of any type. To God be the glory!

My right arm was still immobilized in a sling, and my back was still in excruciating pain. I underwent many radiation treatments to both. The crew at the radiation unit was very friendly. I

Mercy Beyond Measure

was placed on the table and told not to move. Then the friendly faces would disappear, followed by jolts released into the marked areas. I would look at all the heavy equipment, and sometimes I would see the currents, but I really did not have a clue as to what was going on inside me. God's presence dissolves all fears. The technicians observed me from an adjacent room.

In addition to the radiation treatment, I was on high doses of morphine, was wearing a 150-mg Duragesic® patch, and was receiving blood transfusions. After my stay in the hospital, I was moved to an extended-care facility within the hospital grounds, called the *Providence House*. From a biblical standpoint, *Providence* denotes God's sovereignty, the care or benevolent guidance of God as the guiding power of the universe. When God is the head of your life, favors keep coming your way. God rained down supernatural and human favors. Glory to God!

While at the Providence House, physical and occupational therapy was ordered. There was one orthopedic surgeon who wanted to insert a rod in my right arm to help make it mobile, according to him. He was very determined to carry out this procedure. I prayed and reminded my Lord Jesus of Nazareth that I had asked Him to be the head of my life, which means He was responsible for everything concerning my life. I asked Him if a rod would be something that He would recommend. God answered and let me know to tell that doctor to leave me alone.

I spoke with my oncologist and requested that I see another orthopedic surgeon, which she agreed to. Glory to God, the second orthopedic surgeon said that he did not recommend a rod

Mercy Beyond Measure

for my right arm and that it could cause more problems, as the bone was still very fragile. He said the rod might shatter the bone, which was like an eggshell at that point, and that could be disastrous. The doctor recommended that the arm be left alone for a while: three months, for nature to take its course.

The Lord continued to move mightily. Thank you, Lord. Every day my health got better. On January 13, I was discharged to return home.

Mercy Akpan

At Home

The hospital-van driver and my son carried the wheelchair, with me in it, to our upstairs apartment—where a cane, hospital bed, and new wheelchair were waiting for me. There was even a gadget for me to use for reaching or picking up small items.

The hospital bed was much needed because of my back. However, the wheelchair and cane were never used, because my husband stated emphatically that I did not need a wheelchair or cane, adding that I was not old enough yet to call for the use of those things. His other reason was that once a person gets used to using such items, he or she becomes dependent upon them. "Dependency on these things can be very hard to break or wean," my husband would say.

Mercy Beyond Measure

Nurses and therapists were assigned to come check on me. Within a short period of time, the nurses came: first, two days a week; then one day a week. The physical and occupational therapists first came three times a week, and then twice a week. Shortly thereafter, the nurses told me that I was doing well without them, and so they stopped coming.

By March, I had started using my right hand when eating and writing. I had to continue to wear a sling, and the orthopedic surgeon had ordered a specially made arm support for me because the first sling was causing some circulation problems. I bonded with my occupational therapist and my physical therapist, and I shared God's love with them. They were very receptive, and both would ask for prayers. The occupational therapist was a doctoral candidate and would ask for prayer to pass her exams. We would pray together to God, and she did pass all of her exams. I witnessed the glory of the Lord manifest in both of them.

By April, the therapists also terminated their services. By June, I was able to bathe, cook, and shake hands. As for clapping to God in church, it was something I was praying for. Oh, how great God is! He restored me to praise and worship Him!

I also was required to go to the chemotherapy/infusion unit every three to four weeks, to receive Aredia® (pamidronate) to help harden my bones. My understanding of divine healing was this: I thought I would just wake up and not feel any pain. I thought my body would return to how it used to be: no crooked fingers, no compressed spine with protruding bony prominences. I was visualizing a miracle.

The Holy Ghost revealed to me that some healing occurs right away, which is a miracle, but that other healings take place gradually. During the process, God performs an internal cleansing and cleaning. I knew that I would never be the same afterward. As for healing, God has promised and ordered it for you and me. He wrote and executed my treatment plan.

Mercy Akpan

Chemotherapy/Infusion Center: Nightingales

The outpatient infusion room was not just an ordinary one that happened to be located in a hospital facility. Two wonderful, dedicated, and committed caring nurses ran the unit. The love, hugs, and personalized relationships did not go unnoticed. The whole department teamed up and strived to alleviate the somber and lethargic feelings that typically hang over such hospital units. It was never cloudy there, because of this great team. It should come as no surprise, therefore, that Dr. Seetharaman was in charge of this unit as well.

These two nurses termed me a *living miracle*. Both of them, at different times, have said, "When Mercy first came here, she was brought in on a stretcher. She was so sick and had this faraway look. I honestly do believe that she did not know how sick she really was!" How right they were; I knew I was sick, but I did not quite comprehend how seriously ill or critical it was. I had sensed something was seriously wrong, but I was too sick to dwell on it. God had a plan. The following Scripture reinforced my trust and hope in God:

But now thus saith the LORD that created thee, O Jacob, and he that formed thee, O Israel, Fear not: for I have redeemed thee, I have called thee by thy name; Thou art mine. When thou passest through waters, I will be with thee; And through the rivers, they shall not over flow thee: When thou walkest through the fire, thou shalt not be burned; neither shall the flame kindle upon thee. (Isa. 43:1-2)

Above all, I knew that my God had promised to see me through, as He revealed to my pastor before the diagnosis. "Can a woman forget her sucking child, that she should not have compassion on the son of her womb? Yea, they may forget, yet will I not forget thee" (Isa. 49:15).

Mental Warfare

Having addressed my physical attacks and struggles, it is now time to address my mental warfare. Truth and honesty will help encourage you to know that you are not crazy. Cancer diagnoses often create a certain mind-set, even at the mere mention of the word *cancer*. This mind-set is called *fear*, and it must be attacked and dealt with.

The mental warfare was artful, profound, and bold. The intensity of such warfare depends on the level of anointing that God has purposed for you. I would sit in church listening to Pastor Black teach, preach, and pray—only to hear a stupid voice say to me, "Soon he will be preaching at your funeral." I would see a casket with my body in it at the sanctuary base, and people going by to pay their last respects.

If I drove in a car and happened to pass by a funeral home or cemetery, or even a hearse, I would immediately look in the opposite direction. If I dared to look at the location, the devil would attack my mind by telling me that I was going to be laid to rest there soon. Passing the cemetery, the devil would mock, "Guess what? One of these dead people will follow you right now because they know soon you will be one of them."

Seeing a funeral procession, or passing by one, was an entirely different story. Fear would come over me in such a way that I would panic. A voice in my mind would say, "If you are not going to die, you would not have been around that at the time."

Mercy Beyond Measure

It was then that I started hearing that I should not waste my time, for I was going to die. The devil showed me how helpless my sons would be without me. I saw my funeral procession, and I saw my family and friends crying.

I remember one day in particular, when our youngest son had a school assignment for English class, in which he was asked to make up some words. He asked for my help. The first few words that I came up with were *procession, funeral,* and *carnation.* I then suddenly realized, through the love and mercy of my God and the Holy Spirit, what I was saying. I immediately told my son to disregard those words, and he obeyed without question. (We had not even told him yet about the diagnosis.) I prayed and rebuked those thoughts in the name of Jesus.

Temptations poured in. Attacks came out from all angles. Meanwhile, the pain intensified without relief, and the mental warfare magnified and persisted. When I read and studied the Bible and meditated on the goodness of the Lord, my mind was freed. When I sang spiritual hymns, I was freed as well. The moment I stayed away from reading the Bible and praising God, I became a basket case.

I began to ask Jesus, my Lord and Savior, why I was going through such mental warfare. I must tell you that even though I was reading and studying the Bible, I could not memorize and reproduce a line from it. While reading, it seemed as if I had retained the words, but to reproduce them afterward out loud so that the devil would flee was difficult. And to think that I used to memorize entire Shakespearean plays, and never kept an address book or Rolodex, because I locked in phone numbers and license plates numbers in memory. My history essays were never without dates to back up events.

I tried desperately to remember a line of what I had read from the Bible, but to no avail. Yet a soft, sweet voice told me to keep reading. I kept going to church to be filled with the Word, which I did not hide in my heart. I allowed the devil to tamper with my reproduction of the Word of God. I inclined my ear unto God's Word, but I did not allow it to be rooted and grounded deeply in me. I thought I had grasped what I read, but when the time came for me to use those words to contradict the devil, I became clueless.

> My son, attend to my words; incline thine ear unto my sayings.

Let them not depart from thine eyes; keep them in the midst of thine heart.

For they are life unto those that find them, and health to all their flesh. (Prov. 4:20-22)

My worst time was nighttime. I was afraid to go to bed, knowing that I might not wake up. I was afraid to sleep alone—my husband worked nights—but I kept praying and reading the Bible. This mental warfare was intense, cruel, tormenting, and relentless. It was a heavy downpour of fiery darts. I was fear-stricken but not consumed. Despite the intensity of the attacks, God's promise of healing me was always fresh in my heart. Fear gradually started to dwindle away, and the freedom that came upon my soul was beyond description. It is the Word of God that set me free from such mental bondage.

I did not share this with anyone. I could have gone to my pastor for help—believe me, he is always available to his flock—but I decided to take it all to God. To God be all the glory! I thank God for the Holy Spirit, whose burden-removing, yoke-destroying power set me free. "And it shall come to pass in that day, that his burden shall be taken away from off thy shoulder, and his yoke from off thy neck, and the yoke shall be destroyed because of the anointing" (Isa. 10:27).

I pressed on! He was waiting. His garment and arms were wide-open for me, as they are for you. Don't you know that the devil will try to prevent you from receiving your blessings? The devil is not afraid of going through or into anyone to get to you. Recognize it for what it is, no matter whom it has gone into. Remain focused on the Lord, and engross your life in the Word of God.

Guess what? The Holy One, who was sinless, died for our sins and reunited us with God. He won the victory, through his death and resurrection defeated Satan, and has already given us the victory over disease and sickness. Press your way forward toward the mark that will earn you a crown. God wants you to live. He not only wants you alive but also wants you to claim and enjoy your divine inheritance. Begin to praise and worship God, and fill your heart and mind with all of his wondrous works. Think of things that are pure, things that have good reports, and things that have virtue.

Finally, brethren, whatsoever things are true, whatsoever things are honest, whatsoever things are just, whatsoever things are pure, whatsoever things are lovely, whatsoever things are of good report; if there be any virtue, and if there be any praise, think on these things. (Phil. 4:8)

During the mental-warfare phase, I armed myself with some biblical stories, such as the one about the healing and life extension of King Hezekiah:

In those days was Hezekiah sick unto death. And Isaiah the prophet the son of Amoz came unto him, Thus saith the LORD, Set thine house in order: for thou shalt die and not live. Then Hezekiah turned his face toward the wall, and prayed unto the LORD, And said, Remember now, O LORD, I beseech thee, how I have walked before thee in truth and with a perfect heart, and have done that which is good in thy sight. And Hezekiah wept sore. Then came the word of the Lord to Isaiah, saying, Go, and say to Hezekiah, Thus saith the LORD, the God of David thy father, I have heard thy prayer, I have seen thy tears: behold, I will add unto thy days fifteen years. (Isa. 38:1-5)

There is also the story of the woman with the issue of blood, who had to press her way through a great multitude (Mark 5:25-34). In her mind she knew who would make her whole. Do you

Mercy Beyond Measure

know what the multitude consisted of? Serpents, scorpions, and other powers of darkness and principalities. Even the disciples tried to keep her away. I am sure some of her friends were ridiculing her for believing that if she only could touch the hem of His garment, she would be made whole.

The same multitude exists today. Some people might think you are crazy if you say that you believe your healing comes from God and his Anointed One, Jesus. Some people might even conclude that you are suffering because of your sins or the sins of your parents. Do not condemn yourself, nor allow others to judge or condemn you. Be strong. (For more, refer to "Healing a Man Born Blind" [John 9:1-41].)

Some will believe with you for your healing; some will write you off for the dead. Press your way, and press on. He is with you. *Do not give up!* God will deliver what He promised: "For I am the LORD that healeth thee" (Exod. 15:26).

One early morning, I got up to pray. I began, "Lord, I am asking you to know me personally. I want an individual relationship with you, such that when I call on you, I want you to recognize my voice and answer me." I did not finish this prayer, when this response came to me in the form of melody in my dialect:

<u>Nigerian version</u>:

Kot mmi, ke nye yere-e

Kot mmi, ke nye yere-e

Ke usen ubok, nye yere-e

Ke okon eyo, nye yere-e

Eyen kot mmi ke, nye yere-e

Kot mmi, ke nye yere-e

(Repeat twice.)

English version:

Call me, I will answer

Call me, I will answer

In the morning, I will answer

In the night, I will answer

My child, call me and I will answer

It was overwhelming. I was convinced, more than ever, that God was my Father and knew me personally. His answering me back in my native dialect, even though I prayed in English, really astounded me. I believe that God responded in my dialect to show me that the individualized relationship I was asking for was already there and also to show me that He knew me as well as my needs.

God is with me in this fire. He is my strength, my hiding place, my high tower, and high priest. I knew, without a doubt, that I was healed. Hallelujah! By responding in my dialect, it proved to me how intimately He knew me. If you could have seen my heart, you would have understood the peace.

Do not be discouraged. Look up to Jesus, and depend on only him for everything. When you depend on man, you will be very disappointed and hurt. Remember the man at the Beautiful Gate? He waited thirty-eight years for man to help him into the well in order for him to receive healing. Someone took him to the site of the water and left him there, and he could not get into the water after the angel of God had come to

Mercy Beyond Measure

bless the water. He blamed his situation on people. He failed to depend on God.

Depend on Jesus. Jesus Christ will not leave you halfway. From start to finish, He is faithful. You can prolong your illness by yielding to human assistance. The arm of flesh will fail you, but Jesus will never fail you! Set your eyes on Jesus. He is your only source. "I am the way, the truth, and the life" (John 14:6).

Trust no other but Him. He will never fail you. Also remember that God is the only one who can help you. He has infinite ways of accomplishing his will, purpose, and plans for us. He may decide to send someone of the human flesh, but do not worship the person; know that all good things come from God. Thank God for the person, but accord all the glory, adoration, and honor to God.

Remember the story of King Asa of Judah: "And Asa in the thirty and ninth year of his reign was diseased in his feet, until his disease was exceedingly great: yet in his disease he sought not to the LORD but to the physicians. And Asa slept with his fathers, and died in the one and fortieth year of his reign" (2 Chron. 16:12-13).

Watch out: People who never called you before for a long time will come out of the woodwork. They will try to distract you spiritually. Also be alert for the spirits in your church and around you. Some of them will ask how you are doing; then, the moment you respond that you are fine, they immediately say, "Are you sure?" Some even do such a thing right after the pastor has delivered or taught the most stimulating teaching on faith.

Mercy Beyond Measure

It makes you wonder, but please recognize that the serpent is not happy that you are doing fine. It will get into any willing vessel to try to bring doubt and fear to your mind. Have faith and positive bold spirit. You do not have room in your heart for doubt at this time. Cling, cleave unto God. Be deeply rooted and grounded in God. I found out that it is not enough to say, "I'm fine, thank you." You have to retort back with the Word of God, such as saying, "Has God ever lied?" or "God's promises are yeah, and Amen!"

Guess what? You have a perfect opportunity to minister to such people so they too realize that God's Word does not return void until it has accomplished that which He commanded. Ask the Holy Spirit to help you. Make Him your companion, friend, and advisor. He is waiting patiently for you to invite him in.

Do not allow the devil to rob you. Do not entertain offenses, as they come to steal your faith in God. Offenses are the Antichrist and lead to the spirit of strife. You want to clear your mind and keep it clean and fit to communicate with the throne of grace.

Do not be angry with the person. Treat what is said as coming from the pit of hell. Let love overflow from you and out of you. Jehovah-rapha is the healer. There is a blessed assurance when Jehovah heals; you don't worry about a relapse, because He heals and cures at the root, source, and point of origination. Jehovah goes through the complete system—cleansing, purifying, and restoring you. Hallelujah! He is the porter. He knows which bumps, pellets, and pebbles are defective. Jehovah-rapha—that's who He is.

Mercy Beyond Measure

Healing is just one of his many redemptive functions freely given.

The devil would sometimes tell me that I would never use my hand again. I rebuked it in Jesus' name, and I cast it out in Jesus' name. I flooded my time and myself in the Word of God. Of course, the devil was crushed and defeated. "Resist the devil, and he will flee from you" (James 4:7). I no longer wear a sling at home or out in the community.

Thank God for Jesus, who won the battle for us. Victory is ours if we allow God to be sovereign. God will never fail us. He guaranteed us victory and made a public show and shame of the devil. God with His mighty hand delivered the children of Israel out of Egypt.

When my bank account was closed and my life insurance canceled, I ached whenever I looked at my children. I did not have anything to leave behind for them. The devil really capitalized on and magnified my situation. The devil would say, "Now that your insurance has been canceled, I bet you are going to die." On the other hand, the Lord had convinced me that my health was fine.

Whose report would you believe? You must choose to believe the report of the Lord. God does not lie. The devil is the only liar I know. I was in combat, and the Lord was with me. My God is my commander and captain, so I needed to obey his rules. I made up my mind to cling and cleave unto God and his promises. I remained disciplined in my prayer life, positive in my confession, and extremely focused on God's promises. I offered my thoughts and tongue to Christ Jesus. "Death and life are in the power of the tongue" (Prov. 18:21). It is therefore imperative to be extremely conscious of what we say at all times.

If you do not know how to pray, just follow the Lord's Prayer. Start to praise God sincerely for all his wondrous works; sing to him; and then continue to praise him. If you have totally surrendered yourself to him, his faithfulness and glory will circle around you. Speak, sing, worship, and praise him in any language. He created every tongue, so He understands all.

I paid attention when I read the Bible. Every time before I began reading, I would say a short prayer, asking the Holy Spirit to impart wisdom, understanding, revelation, and knowledge to me. I would ask God to reveal the true meaning as He intended for his Word to benefit me in my walk with him, and to reveal the situation or circumstance that I was facing. Then I would begin reading, and my prayer was answered every time.

The Holy Spirit would reveal some startling things to me. One such Scripture read, "This sickness is not unto death, but for the glory of God, that the Son of God might be glorified thereby" (John 11:4). Something rose up within me when I came across this verse. I was told to look at the words, followed by a voice saying, "This is for you...Don't worry. Be still!"

Another Scripture that touched me deeply read, "Surely goodness and mercy shall follow me all the days of my life: and I will dwell in the house of the LORD forever" (Ps. 23:6). When I read those words, a whole new world of freedom began to unfold for me. I then realized that all believers are destined and guaranteed good things: health, wealth, peace, joy, and the like.

The Holy Spirit began to minister to me, using a very personal incident. My father had developed a severe cardiac ailment, which had caused him to vomit cupfuls of blood. Upon arrival at the hospital, the doctor told my oldest brother that my father was losing blood from his heart and was living on only three-quarters of his heart capacity. Therefore, he would live for only six months, and there was not much they could do for him. My father was discharged on Christmas Eve 1958, and we all went to my village, as it was the tradition for all of us to be at home for a big Christmas celebration. To God's glory, my father was healed of this ailment, and he lived productively until 1982.

The faith and trust I witnessed from my father's experiences strengthened me to persevere. I kept hearing, "The symptoms and feeling will disappear gradually." I began to reflect on the various symptoms and feelings that I was no longer experiencing (e.g., severe chest pains, and dizziness). God increased my faith. The slogan "This too shall pass in the name of Jesus" was branded on my heart.

Other attacks and fiery darts were aimed at me. The Lord healed me of shingles, a stomach virus, insomnia, and pneumonia, plus other things that only He will ever know. Through my pain, God assured me that I would be all right. I do not even have scars from the shingles. Glory to God!

I also know that just before we receive our blessing, the devil really unleashes attacks on us. When comfort seems to come, discomfort swells. After a while, my blood work began to spin out of control, and my wonderful, gentle, and sweet oncologist began to worry. She concluded that she would give me chemotherapy and would schedule that a port be inserted for the administration of this *cocktail*, as she called it.

As I was walking through the hospital to the lab to have blood drawn for presurgery evaluation, I heard a soft voice say, "Ask those nurses at the chemo infusion room about this cocktail that your doctor is talking about, because it is poison." I walked straight to the chemo outpatient unit and asked the nurses. They took turns responding: "Why does she want to give you that?"; "Do you know what is in those drugs?"; "You don't need that"; "I can't believe she would want you on that stuff...Did you ask her why?"

I told them that my doctor was concerned about the continuous increase of the bad protein in my blood and that she said the medicine was not bad, because I would be given very small doses of each drug. I asked them for a printout of the facts about the three drugs that were going to be combined to make up this so-called cocktail. I glanced through the information and then asked the nurses to please tell my doctor to call me at home that night—no matter how late.

Then I went for my blood work. You might wonder why I went. I like to make a boast in my Lord, and one of the ways I do this is by allowing God to complete his course by confounding unbelievers. Well, at the lab, after three failed attempts to draw blood from different sites on both arms, the technician did not have enough to use for any of the tests. She said, "I don't understand this...I'm not going to stick you anymore." So I left and returned home to wait for the phone call.

The doctor called me that evening, and I expressed my concerns. She apologized and told me not to proceed for the surgery but to come to her first thing Monday morning to explore some other options. It was not her intention to scare me.

I went on Monday to see her, and she totally abandoned the idea of the cocktail. Doing so opened a door for her to be able to obtain a trial drug, and I was the first person to receive it. She had previously tried to obtain this drug for use on another patient, but she could not gain approval. God's favor made a way for me, and she said later, "I can't believe how easily everything worked out." God purified my blood and delivered me from the poison.

> Many are the afflictions of the righteous: but the Lord delivereth him out of them all. (Ps. 34:19)

> He keepeth all his bones: not one of them is broken. (Ps. 34:19-20)

On February 4, 2000, my doctor confirmed that as far as the disease was concerned, my body was free. My organs were in good health. Giving me back to my family was a good gift, but the best gift of all was the intimacy that He enabled me to have with Him. The greatest legacy of this wonderful journey was the fact that

Mercy Beyond Measure

God, out of grace and mercy, called me and recruited me into his army. Almighty God has chosen me to be in his royal priesthood, a holy nation, and a peculiar person. To God be all the honor, glory, and praise forever more. Such agape love! It is humbling.

Realize that God will not give us more than we can bear:

> There hath no temptation taken you but such as is common to man: but God is faithful, who will not suffer you to be tempted above that ye are able; but will with the temptation also make a way to escape, that ye may be able to bear it. (1 Cor. 10:13)

Forasmuch then as the children are partakers of flesh and blood, he also himself likewise took part of the same; that through death he might destroy him that had the power of death, that is, the devil; And deliver them who through fear of death were all their lifetime subject to bondage. For verily he took not on him the nature of angels; but he took on him the seed of Abraham. Wherefore in all things it behooved him to be made like unto his brethren, that he might be a merciful and faithful high priest in things pertaining to God, to make reconciliation for the sins of the people. For in that he himself suffered being tempted, he is able to succor them that are tempted. (Heb. 2:14-18)

You are an overcomer, because of Jesus Christ: "Weeping may endure for a night, but joy cometh in the morning" (Ps. 30:5). Engross yourself in the Word of God. Praise and worship Him. Focus on Him. The following Scripture sums it up:

> Looking unto Jesus the author and finisher of our faith; who for the joy that was set before him endured the cross, despising the shame, and is set down at the right hand of the throne of God. For consider Him that endured such contradiction of sinners against himself, lest ye be wearied and faint in your minds. (Heb. 12:2-3)

Face your fear head-on, and identify it. Refocus on positiveness, and avoid pity parties. Refuse and resist those things and people that will drag you down. Fall in love with Jesus Christ. Seek the things of the Kingdom of God, and begin to walk in divine direction. Yield for total cleansing and purging. You will receive your healing in Jesus' name.

I must emphasize that healing is both spiritual and physical. Your heart must belong to God. A word from my heart: Be patient, prayerful, and trusting. No matter what it is, trust that God's will is best for you, and surrender your life to God. He will make sure that his will and purpose for you have been fulfilled, and nothing shall prevail against that will. "For I know the thoughts that I think toward you, saith the LORD, thoughts of peace, and not of evil, to give you an expected end" (Jer. 29:11).

Remember that Jesus defeated death and gained eternal life for all who believed in him. It is God's will that we are well, and it is also his will to heal us should we become ill. Jesus healed all that were sick who came to him. A lot of people have been healed, and many more will receive healing in Jesus' name. Strive toward godly living, and call unto God, and remain constant and committed in seeking him. "Call unto me, and I will answer thee, and show thee great and mighty things, which thou knowest not" (Jer. 33:3).

God wants us to be in good health, not only physical but also spiritual. It is therefore imperative to know how to receive our healing and how to hold onto it. Faith is the key to keeping this precious gift of healing from our Savior and Lord Jesus Christ. Stay in the Word. Praise, worship, and pray always. Give your tongue and thoughts to God.

Yes, there are some who can simply walk into a church or healing crusade and become instantly healed, some without any church affiliation. But there are also some who have to go through discipline spiritually to receive this Christ-earned gift. Whatever the strategy may be, rest assured that God—through his only begotten Son, Jesus—gave us the right to good health and more. In order to be complete and be made whole, be patient and believe. Allow God to work in you, inside and out.

It is so good to be spiritually and physically healed. This is divine wholesomeness. You will be delivered from the bondage of fear, as I was. The apostle Paul clearly states, "We are confident, I say, and willing rather to be absent from the body, and to be present with the Lord. Wherefore we labor, that, whether present or absent, we may be accepted of him" (2 Cor. 5:8-9).

God will strengthen you, so depend and trust in him alone. Pray, pray, and pray. Remember that prayer changes things. Even when it looks like God has not heard you, continue to pray. As you seek and pray diligently, God prepares you for things. What was once unbearable becomes bearable and insignificant. Be patient. Pray for others.

Sometimes God might decide to stop by to bless some other person before coming to you. He has not forgotten about you, and He arrives at the right time. Jesus loved Lazarus so much, but He tarried two days after He heard of his death, and arrived on time to raise him up. Persist, persist, and persist. Do not give up if your first cry or plea does not get God's attention. Cry the more, and wrestle the more, and be specific in your request. Jacob wrestled with God for His blessing (Gen. 32:26).

God sees and knows our hearts, intentions, and motives. He never forgot your case. He is in it with you; He is on it; and He is working on you internally until his Word is accomplished.

Resist all the lies that the devil brings—bearing in mind that those who observe lying vanities forsake their own mercies. Remember that prayer is your communication link to your heavenly Father. Oh, how He enjoys this time with you.

When your skin is dry, you must moisturize it. You apply the moisturizer until the flakes disappear. Prayer is the moisturizer, and you become dry and scaly without it. You must always stay in the Word of God. Meditate and pray until it is embedded in you. You must pray until you have a breakthrough, or until something happens. You are so precious and special to Him.

Step and stump on the liar's head, and do not get off until you have squeezed the brain out completely and have beaten its remains to powdered dust. Do not leave its dust in a pile or heap, lest it regroups and strikes again. Pour gasoline, kerosene, or any combustible liquid on it, and burn it.

The Word of God is your weapon. Read. Study. Be rooted and grounded in the Word of God. Have your child, husband, friend, or believer read to you. Listen to anointed tapes, and praise hymns. Praise God, and exalt his holy name.

We must not forget to look after the body, which is God's temple. It is not uncommon for us to lose the appetite and desire to eat when we are sick. Satan also plays a major role in this area—knowing that without food, there is no physical strength. When our Lord Jesus raised up Jairus's daughter, He ordered that she be fed (plus other instructions).

Lack of food diminishes the immune system and therefore makes you susceptible to various forms of infections. When you are physically weak, Satan knows it. How can you pray exhausted? Proper nutrition is mandatory. During my period of attack, I experienced a severe loss of appetite, but God delivered me, and he will deliver you. Glory to his holy name.

Mercy Beyond Measure

First of all, I know that my problem came mostly from food additives and preservatives. Therefore, I sought divine guidance regarding what to eat and what to avoid. Returning 100 percent to basics was not an option. I ate my ancestral foods. I consumed foods that were mostly in their natural, wholesome forms (e.g., leafy green vegetables, and beans). I always enjoy well-prepared beans, like my mother used to make. My mother was a silent unsung divine general. She was the best mother and cook in the world.

I also ate a lot of fish (with scales). I also included chicken but ate it sparingly. I eliminated sugar. I still ate fruits but did not go overboard, because of their sugar content. Cancer cells thrive well and multiply when there is an abundance of sweets. I drank a lot of good natural water, with a preference for distilled water during the period of convalescence.

Use whatever works for you; pray over anything that you consume; and believe that our Lord watches over us. He alone is the greatest physician and healer. Healing comes from God and God only. Yield totally for a makeover only possible by God. Seek spiritual healing first. "But seek ye first the kingdom of God, and his righteousness; and all these things shall be added unto you" (Matt. 6:33).

If you haven't been eating, get up and eat. Don't dwell on the lack of taste or the bloated feeling; just eat something healthy, no matter how small. It could be a bite this time, and gradually the bite will increase. Many times it is not the disease that kills, but rather how we

Mercy Beyond Measure

allow our situation and environment to impact us.

Every rose has a thorn, but we can pick the flower without being pricked. No matter what your environment is, no matter how sweet or rotten your relationship is with your loved ones or friends, no matter the social and economic situation, do not allow any carnal conditions dictate to you how you are going to fight this warfare. Remember that this is your life. Trust God and God only.

If your situation is good, and the people around you are there to answer every call of yours, thank God and enjoy it. However, if you are faced with an adverse situation without support, love, and all other fleshly enticement, do not allow these to impact you. I am not saying it does not hurt, especially if you have been supportive. Remember that the devil wants you dead, and so it will do everything to weaken you spiritually.

God will raise up people to be there for you. Do not worry if your spouse should fail you, for He will make it so your children, friends, or strangers are there for you. Some friends will try to hurt you; such people were not friends in the first place. As painful as this might be, it is good to experience now, as it will build and strengthen your faith, trust, and dependency in only God.

No matter what you are going through, I just want you to know that the Saving Light is about to shine for you. It has always been shining for you, but now is the time for you to enjoy the illumination of this Light. You might ask, "Who is this person? How can she know what I'm going through?" You are perfectly right in your

Mercy Beyond Measure

questioning, but have an open mind, and you will come to the full understanding that no matter what it is, you are set toward the reaping of your freedom. You must believe that with God, all things are possible. "For we walk by faith, not by sight" (2 Cor. 5:7).

When you love someone, you trust that person. You cannot love without trust and belief. People often die from the fear of disease rather than from the actual disease. Fear is the opposite of faith. Sight is also the opposite of faith. Your mind becomes a battleground, which can be tormenting. You tightly shut your eyes, hoping the voice of the wicked one will vanish. No! No! No! It is adamant and stubborn to all carnal interventions.

Only one thing and one thing only can get rid of this monster called *fear*: the Word of God. You must know the Word and live it. Ask God for faith.

> Now faith is the substance of things hoped for, the evidence of things not seen. For by it the elders obtained a good report. Through faith we understand that the worlds were framed by the word of God, so that things which are seen were not made of things which do appear. But without faith it is impossible to please him: for he that cometh to God must believe that he is, and that he is a rewarder of them that diligently seek him. (Heb. 11:1-2, 6)

It is imperative to have faith in God, for He is the cornerstone and foundation of the anointing. Faith in God holds the key to receiving. By faith,

Mercy Beyond Measure

Abraham became the father of many nations when he was about one hundred years old. By faith, Sarah conceived and bore Isaac at an age when it was humanly impossible. Abraham had no room for unbelief:

Who against hope believed in hope, that he might become the father of many nations, according to that which was spoken, SO SHALL THY SEED BE. And being not weak in faith, he considered not his own body now dead, when he was about an hundred years old, neither yet the deadness of Sarah's womb: He staggered not at the promise of God through unbelief; but was strong in faith, giving glory to God; And being fully persuaded that, what he had promised, he was able also to perform. And therefore IT WAS IMPUTED TO HIM FOR RIGHTEOUSNESS. Now it was not written for his sake alone, that it was implied to him; But for us also, to whom it shall be imputed, if we believe on him that raised up Jesus our Lord from the dead; Who was delivered for our offences, and was raised again for our justification. (Rom. 4:18-25)

By faith, the children of Israel passed through the Red Sea as by dry land. Many mighty works took place because of faith in God, and they still are taking place today for the very same reason. God loves us so much, but do we love him in return? If we do love God, we should trust and believe in him. His promises to us are awesome, and He has never reneged on any of his promises—of which healing is one of them.

Whatever you are facing...

> If the doctor has handed you a no-hope diagnosis
>
> If you are locked up in darkness
>
> If you are alone among the midst of uncaring people
>
> If you are in a jail cell
>
> If your family is falling apart

...look up and believe that God is your deliverer. Be set free!

Are you ready? Are you ready...

> for deliverance?
>
> for freedom?
>
> for peace?

for joy?

for liberty?

Hallelujah! Say yes, yes, yes! Say, "I have been freed because of Jesus!"

> But they that wait upon the Lord shall renew their strength; they shall mount up with wings as eagles; they shall run, and not be weary; and they shall walk, and not faint. (Isa. 40:31)

Are you beginning to feel liberated? You feel like bursting loose? Good, praise Him, because it means you are sick and tired of being deprived of all your blessings. When praises go up, blessings come down! Worship Him. He is worthy.

You must begin to eradicate those little wrinkles, spots, debris, and blemishes that the devil has been speaking to you about, and get rid of the weights, resentment, and unforgivingness. It is like exhaling and inhaling: You exhale carbon dioxide, and you inhale oxygen; you exhale what is bad, and you inhale what is good to repair and heal your tissues.

Ready to begin? If you are thirsty, frustrated, tired, and hungry, and your attitude is one of "I have had it," then this is for you. You must ask Jesus to come into your life. What you gain in the long run is a permanent road to internal freedom and joy, plus an external divine makeover, everlasting glory, and eternal life.

Salvation is for all, and you must believe that God sent Jesus to redeem us through his suffering, death, crucifixion, resurrection, and ascension. Jesus is seated at the right hand of God the Father, and Jesus will return again for us. What a difference this makes. We are His coheirs; therefore, all that God the Father has given Jesus, we will share.

You see, I am sharing with you how and why I have come to the stage of freedom, joy, and peace, and how I was able to receive not only physical healing but also spiritual healing. He did it for me; He is continually doing it for all who believe in him; and He is ready to do it for you. He is calling you. His arms are open. He is waiting patiently for you. Just invite Him into your heart, and begin to drink from the fountain of everlasting life.

> Behold, I stand at the door, and knock: if any man hear my voice, and open the door, I will come in to him, and will sup with him, and he with me. (Rev. 3:20)

Mercy Beyond Measure

That if thou shalt confess with thy mouth the Lord Jesus, and shalt believe in thine heart that God hath raised him from the dead, thou shalt be saved. For with the heart man believeth unto righteousness; and with the mouth confession is made unto salvation. For the scripture saith, WHOSOEVER BELIEVETH ON HIM SHALL NOT BE ASHAMED. (Rom. 10:9-11)

People often say, "What you do not know does not hurt you." This may hold some truth in the earth realm. In the spiritual realm, however, spiritual blindness is extremely dangerous and frightening. What you do not know *will* hurt you. "My people are destroyed for lack of knowledge" (Hos. 4:6).

When you have Jesus in your life, and you yield to his lordship, blessings will overtake you. He will direct your paths, as you observe God's commandments and virtues and strive toward righteousness. No one can love and treat you like Jesus can.

Though salvation is for all, ask God to help you go beyond the outer court. Intimacy with God is like schoolwork. If you want to be an A student, you must present work above B students. The harder you work by studying and being teachable, the further you will progress. Do not be satisfied at the outer court. Strive to travel to the inner court, and then remain in continuous communion.

This is intimacy, and God shares his will, purpose, and ways through the Holy Spirit. Here you can call those things that are not as though they were.

Guard Your Healing: Affliction Will Not Return Twice

There are many factors that will help maintain your wholesomeness and well-being once Jesus, the Anointed One, has touched and healed your body. You must be vigilant in the spirit to discern those things.

If people become willing to share or confide in you, beware. That is the time to ask God to heighten your discerning gift and to fine-tune it. The devil goes overboard at such times. Some of what you will be called for—or the "I'm just confiding in you" issues—will be so full of filth and dirt that these only will clutter your mind and spirit. Shut this door immediately, and engross yourself in the Bible, the Word of God,

Mercy Beyond Measure

which is the only truth. Ask God for the wisdom and filling of the Holy Spirit.

Please bear in mind that the symptoms or pain, which are often experienced after someone has received a touch or healing from God, does not mean that you are not healed. These are just distractions to confuse you. Keep up your prayer life, and keep reading and studying the Bible. Do not question or doubt, as this will definitely open the door for the manipulator to return. Walk in love and forgiveness. Renew your mind toward the Kingdom's purposes and plans. Praise God. Publicly give Him a Thanksgiving.

When you hope for something, you must exercise patience, and you must believe. During such a time, do not take your eyes off the promise. Fellowship with fellow believers who have like minds toward Jesus, who go to church, who pray, and who fast. Sew faithfully and joyfully. Prayer can never hurt you. There is no such thing as praying too much. Jesus prayed always, and He prayed for us (John 17:1-26).

Fasting empowers you. Before you do it, however, check with your doctor. Until you are strong enough to fast for an extended period of time, you can fast for only one hour or just give up something that you like to do (e.g., watching television).

Faith and patience will bring this to pass. Hold on! Hold on! While holding on, enjoy the peace of God. Doing so will keep you from worrying. When I say *patience*, I'm not advocating that you sit back idly and allow the devil to throw mud or clay and punches at you. You must be violent in the spirit, and command the spirit of sickness and bondage to flee your body and mind. Take authority over the situation in the name of Jesus Christ.

Remember to firmly position your feet on solid ground, and the peace of God will prevail. Trust, believe, and pray, and you will be rewarded. God respects everyone. There is no discrimination in Him. No disease should be taken lightly. As a believer and beloved of the Lord, it is best to arm yourself with the faithfulness and Word of God.

God Almighty delivered Shadrach, Meshach, and Abednego. Cancer is Nebuchadnezzar, Egypt, and the Pharaoh. God Almighty delivered His people from these enemies. "Be strong and courageous, be not afraid nor dismayed for the King of Assyria, nor for all the multitude that is with him: for there be more with us than with him: With him is an arm of flesh; but with us is the Lord our God to help us, and to fight our battles" (2 Chron. 32:7-8).

Nebuchadnezzar commanded that the furnace be heated seven times more than usual and that the most-mighty men of his army were to bind Shadrach, Meshach, and Abednego, and cast them into the burning fiery furnace. God delivered them (Dan. 3:1-30). Jesus Christ is the same yesterday, today, and forever (Heb. 13:8).

No matter what you are going through, flood your mind with the Word of God. Cleave and cling unto God. Call unto Jesus, the Anointed One, and know that by His stripes you were healed. God is your Healer. He is the only one who knows your frame. He created you; therefore, it is fair to say that He is the only one who can heal you, because He knows you. He heals from the root origin. He makes you whole.

Mercy Beyond Measure

Doctors go after only symptoms. I am not undermining doctors; there are some very good ones, and God uses those who seek His guidance and counsel. Pray for such ones. He gave me one, and He will give you one.

Behold, I have graven thee upon the palms of my hands; thy walls are continually before me. (Isa. 49:16)

Are not two sparrows sold for a farthing? And one of them shall not fall on the ground without your Father. But the very hairs of your head are all numbered. Fear ye not therefore, ye are of more value than many sparrows. (Matt. 10:29-31)

God so loves us so much that He chose to send his beloved and only Son to redeem us from darkness into the Kingdom of Light. God knew that it would not be an easy job and realized that in order to defeat such a formidable enemy, it would take no other but his Son to accomplish the task. He stepped from the realm of his heavenly throne and transformed himself into the likeness of man to come and do the job himself. He shed his Precious Blood to give us salvation, peace, joy, and eternal life. He defeated Satan and won healing for us. Glory to God!

God does not lie. He delivers all that He has promised. His words and promises are authentic.

God's love and kindness are immeasurable. It is impossible for me to recount all of the mercies that God has given me, as they are unending. "It is of the LORD's mercies that we are not consumed, because his compassions fail not. They are new every morning: great is thy faithfulness" (Lam. 3:22-23). God's mercies toward me are countless, abundant, and overflowing. His mercies started long before my parents obeyed his order to allow me to come to be. I thank Him sincerely.

Mercy Akpan

Conclusion

I prayed to God to make it possible for me to someday return to Florida to see that doctor—the one who faithlessly told my husband, "If I were you, I would take the next available plane home." I wanted him to see that God is able to give strength and hope when man has given up, as he had.

God answered my prayer. My husband and I went to see this doctor, and what followed confirmed the unquestionable sovereignty of God. Upon our arrival, one of the nurses who had helped me greeted us. She was in awe: "Oh my God! Look at you. If someone had told me that you would be here today alive, I would not have believed it. Do you know that you are a miracle? You are a walking miracle!" Yes, I do know, and that is why I give God the glory every day, with my hands lifted up.

We next visited with the male nurse who had administered my infusions. He was absolutely delighted to see us. He hugged me and kissed me on the cheek. He spoke from the innermost part of his heart: "You look so good. You look so good." I said it was by the grace of God.

Next stop was the room where I used to receive the infusions. There were at least ten people: some receiving their infusion, some waiting for the same male nurse to start their infusions. I started to explain that I used to sit in one of those seats three-plus years ago, receiving an infusion. I had barely finished my sentence, when God opened the door of utterance to glorify and magnify His name: A woman asked, "What

Mercy Beyond Measure

happened to you? I have to hear, because you look so healthy."

The Holy Spirit quickened me to seize the moment. I told the woman, and several others around her, about my diagnosis and how I had refused conventional treatment because the first oncologist had given me two to three months to live. I mentioned the doctor who told my husband to take me on the next available plane home—surely because he did not want me dying on his premises.

I added, "There were two doctors who had written me off, but God said, 'No, it is not your time yet. Do not put your trust in the liquid you are receiving. Place all your faith and trust in me.' He created us, and loves us so much. Cleave and cling unto Him, and Him alone. He did it for me, not because of anything good that I have done, but because of his grace and mercy. He respects all persons. I just want to encourage you. May God bless you all." The room fell silent when I had concluded what God had commanded to say to them.

Then it was time to see the doctor. He was with a patient but stood completely motionless the moment he saw me. After a wordless exchange, I asked him if he recognized me. He slowly spoke, as though answering a ghost, "Of course I do." Those were his only words, yet his eyes said much more: He was amazed that I was alive.

Two weeks after we returned from Florida, my back was hunched as a result of the compression of my spine. I had prayed that God would straighten it. Just as I was beginning to accept this as a reminder scar of victory for God

Mercy Beyond Measure

and from the battle of cancer, I had a vivid dream, in which I was asked to pray for a man who was dying.

I had two other people with me, and we went to pray for the man. His wife greeted us and directed us to the room where her husband was. He was in a supine position covered with a white sheet. As I stretched my right hand over him and began to pray in the name of Jesus, the man got up from his bed and stood on his feet. He then turned to me and asked me to kneel, which I did, and to put both my hands in front of me. I again did as he requested. He then placed his palms under me and pulled up on my trunk once. I heard a crackling sound. He released me and said, "Get up and look at your back...It is straight now." I opened my eyes.

Two or three days later, I looked at my back in the mirror, and the hunched area was straight. I took the dream as a message that I must go out to pray and encourage others who are afflicted. As I minister to them in the name of Jesus, God will heal them, and I will continue to walk in divine health. As we believe and trust in God and his Son, Jesus Christ, we begin to enjoy the downpour and overflow of His infinite mercies. After years of facing a fiery furnace, I can honestly say this: "I shall not die, but live, and declare the works of the LORD" (Ps. 118:17).

To God be all the glory!

Appendix A

Enjoy the following healing Scriptures, all of which are from the Authorized (King James) Version of the Bible. Meditate on them daily and as often as you can, anyplace and anytime.

Beloved, I wish above all things that thou mayest prosper and be in health, even as thy soul prospereth. (3 John 2)

How God anointed Jesus of Nazareth with the Holy Ghost and with power: who went about doing good, and healing all that were oppressed of the devil; for God was with him. (Acts 10:38)

He sent His word, and healed them, and delivered them, from their destructions. (Ps. 107:20)

My son, attend to my words; incline thine ear unto my saying. Let them not depart from thine eyes; keep them in the midst of thine heart. For they are life unto those that find them, and health to all their flesh. (Prov. 4:20-22)

Bless the LORD, o my soul: and forget not all his benefits: who for giveth all thine iniquities; who healeth all thy diseases; who redeemeth thy life from destruction; who crowneth thee with loving kindness and tender mercies; who satisfieth thy mouth with good things; so that thy youth is renewed like the eagle's. (Ps. 103:2-5)

Who his own self bare our sins in His own body on the tree, that we, being dead to sins, should live unto righteousness: BY WHOSE STRIPES YE WERE HEALED. (1 Pet. 2:24)

And Jesus went about all Galilee, teaching in their synagogues, and preaching the gospel of the kingdom, and healing all manner of sickness and all manner of disease among the people. And his fame went through out all Syria: and they brought unto him all sick people that were taken with divers diseases and torments, and those which were possessed with devils, and those which were lunatick, and those that had the palsy; and He healed them. (Matt. 4:23-24)

I will come and heal him. (Matt. 8:7)

Thou dumb and deaf spirit, I charge thee, come out of him, and enter no more into him. (Mark 9:25)

And when he had called unto him his twelve disciples, he gave them power against unclean spirits, to cast them out, and to heal all manner of sickness and all manner of disease. (Matt. 10:1)

And to have *power* to heal sickness, and to cast out devils. (Mark 3:15)

Then he called his twelve disciples together, and gave them power and authority over all devils, and to cure diseases. And he sent them to preach the kingdom of God, and to heal the sick. (Luke 9:1-2)

And great multitudes followed him; and he healed them there. (Matt. 19:2)

And the people, when they knew it, followed him: and he received them, and spoke unto them of the kingdom of God, and healed them that had need of healing. (Luke 9:11)

And, behold, there was a certain man before him which had the dropsy. (Luke 14:2)

And he took him, and healed him, and let him go. (Luke 14:2)

And Jesus answered and said, Suffer ye thus far. And He touched his ear, and healed him. (Luke 22:51)

I am the Lord that healeth thee. (Exod. 15:26)

And ye shall serve the Lord your God, and he shall bless thy bread, and thy water; and I will take sickness away from the midst of thee. There shall nothing cast their young, nor be barren in thy land: the number of thy days I will fulfill. (Exod. 23:25-26)

There shall no evil befall thee, neither shall any plague come nigh thy dwelling. (Ps. 91:10)

Because he hath set his love upon me, therefore will I deliver him: I will set him on high, because he hath known my name. (Ps. 91:14)

With long life will I satisfy him, and show him my salvation. (Ps. 91:16)

Surely he hath borne our grief, and carried our sorrows: yet we did esteem him stricken, smitten of God, and afflicted. But he was wounded for our transgressions, he was bruised for our iniquities: the chastisement of our peace was upon him; and with his stripes we are healed. (Isa. 53:4-5)

Appendix B

As you read the following miracles of our Lord, you will be strengthened and encouraged beyond your imagination:

The First Miracle:

Water Made Wine	John 2:1
Many Healings	Matthew 4:23, 8:16, 15:30
	Mark 1:32
	Luke 4:40
A Leper	Matthew 8:1-4
	Mark 1:40
	Luke 5:12-16
The Centurion's Servant	Matthew 8:5
	Luke 7:1

Peter's Wife's Mother   Matthew 8:14

                                         Mark 1:29

                                         Luke 4:38

The Tempest Stilled   Matthew 8:23

                                         Mark 4:35

                                         Luke 8:22

Two Demoniacs   Matthew 8:28

                                         Mark 5:1

                                         Luke 5:18

A Paralytic Man   Matthew 9:1

                                         Mark 2:1

                                         Luke 5:18

Woman with the

Issue of Blood   Matthew 9:20

                                         Mark 5:25

                                         Luke 8:43

Raising of Jairus's Daughter	Matthew 9:23
	Mark 5:22
	Luke 8:41
Two Blind Men	Matthew 9:27
A Dumb Demoniac	Matthew 9:32, 12:22
	Luke 14
A Man with a Withered Hand	Matthew 12:10
	Mark 3:1
	Luke 6:6
Five Thousand Fed	Matthew 14:15
	Mark 6:35
	Luke 9:12
	John 6:1
Jesus Walks on the Sea	Matthew 14:22
	Mark 6:47
	John 6:16

Mercy Akpan

The Syrophenician's Daughter	Matthew 15:21
	Mark 7:24
Four Thousand Fed	Matthew 15:32
	Mark 8:1
The Epileptic Boy	Matthew 17:14
	Mark 9:14
	Luke 9:37
Two Blind Men (Jericho)	Matthew 20:30
A Man with an Unclean Spirit	Mark 1:23
	Luke 4:33
A Deaf Mute	Mark 7:31
A Blind Man (Bethesda)	Mark 8:22
Blind Bartimaeus	Mark 10:46
	Luke 18:35
	Matthew 20:30
Draught of Fishes	Luke 5:4

Raising of Widow's Son	Luke 7:11
An Infirm Woman	Luke 13:11
A Dropsical Man	Luke 14:1
Ten Lepers	Luke 17:11
Malchus's Ear Healed	Luke 22:50
A Noble Man's Son	John 4:46
A Cripple (Bethesda)	John 5:1
A Man Born Blind	John 9:1
Raising of Lazarus	John 11:38
A Great Haul of Fishes	John 21:1

Notes

Mercy Beyond Measure

Notes

Notes

About the Author

Mercy Otu-Etim Akpan presently has been commissioned as an officer of Hesed Foundation, Inc. (www.HesedFoundation.org) in Shrewsbury, Massachusetts, established exclusively for charitable and educational purposes; ministering and providing faith based and clinical ministering counseling and stabilization support services to the elderly, sick, the needy, the homeless, and the general public. Diagnosed with cancer (multiple myeloma) in 1995, with every grim outlook spelled out by the oncologist, "We are talking two to three months you could be dead." In 2002 there is no statement that holds more truth as, "It is of the Lord's mercies that we are not consumed, because his compassions fail not." — Lamentations 3:22

God has commissioned me to share the truth of His loving kindness to a world racked with chaos, confusion, and disbelief. A former co-chairperson and chairperson for Christians Fighting Cancer she is dedicated to spreading divine loving kindness empowerment daily by visits, and phone calls. Mercy, an American originally from Africa, lives in Massachusetts with her husband and two sons.